WITHIN THE FRINGE

Within the Fringe

An Autobiography

JAMES STUART

(Viscount Stuart of Findhorn, PC, CH, MVO, MC)

THE BODLEY HEAD

LONDON   SYDNEY   TORONTO

To Alexander Stuart Frere

ACKNOWLEDGMENTS

I would like to acknowledge my indebtedness to my old friend A. Stuart Frere for the encouragement—not to say prodding—which caused this book to be written, and to another old friend, Alec Douglas-Home, who has provided it with a typically felicitous (and flattering) foreword. I must also pay tribute to the encouragement I have received throughout from my good friends the Herbert Agars and from Norman Brook, one-time Secretary to the Cabinet and now Lord Normanbrook.

I am also grateful to Stephen Watts who, on behalf of The Bodley Head, gave me the benefit of his professional experience in putting the largely undocumented recollections of a lifetime into the form of a book. His help has been invaluable.

Acknowledgment is also due to Randolph Churchill, as an executor of the Churchill estate, for permission to reproduce a letter and a memorandum written to me by his father, and to Sir Alan Herbert, for allowing me to publish some of his verses.

J. S.

The print of the 1st Earl of Moray is reproduced by courtesy of the Duke of Hamilton and the Edinburgh pictures by arrangement with the Radio Times Hulton Picture Library and the *Scotsman*.

Quotations from the lyrics of songs in Chapter V are reproduced by permission as follows: *Blighty* by permission of B. Feldman and Co. Ltd; *I'll Make a Man of You* and *Gilbert the Filbert* by permission of Francis, Day and Hunter Ltd; *The Constant Lover* by permission of Boosey and Hawkes Music Publishers Ltd; and *Goodbye Girls* by permission of Chappell and Co. Ltd.

Contents

Foreword by Sir Alec Douglas-Home, xi

I Introduction – the bastard Earl of Moray – life
with father – schoolboy to soldier, 1

II The First World War – the mood of 1914 – the
Royal Scots – the battle of the Somme, 1916 –
a Military Cross, 4

III An ambition realised – Arras – Bar to M.C. – the
third battle of Ypres, 1917 – 'desertion towards
the enemy' – the *putsch* at Albert, 17

IV Haig and Foch – Armistice – Brussels, 1919 – two
princes and 'The Merry Grill', 25

V Footnotes to the First World War – London
music-halls – Paris leave – Zena Dare, 29

VI Edinburgh – reading for the Bar – golf – Equerry
to the Duke of York, 39

VII Buckingham Palace – tennis with Princess Mary –
the 'new niece' at Ascot – miserable mistakes –
the Duke's character – the oddities of Dick
Molyneux – duty at Balmoral, 44

VIII To New York on the *Aquitania* – Mrs Cornelius
Vanderbilt – encounter with an adding machine –
Oklahoma – oil-drilling etiquette – Gladys
Cooper, 58

IX Home on leave – marriage, 1923 – a surprise
election result – Lord Balfour – Stanley Baldwin
– Scottish Whip, 1935, 69

X Life as a Whip – Nancy, Lady Astor – Neville
and Austen Chamberlain – the 'men of Munich',
79

XI The Buggins principle – Chief Whip, 1941 – working with Churchill, 88

XII Churchill as war-time leader – his extraordinary qualities – Churchilliana – Brendan Bracken – a 'small refreshment', 95

XIII Winston at ease – party conference – Stuarts and Hanoverians – A. P. Herbert – Stafford Cripps – speech-making – Winston on a grouse moor – the need to be a 'butcher' – Parliamentary questions, 111

XIV Churchill's tales of the Kremlin – Stalin, Molotov and the Bolshoi – trouble with Beaverbrook, 129

XV The Caretaker Government – in Opposition, 1945 – Labour bullying – a call on Nye Bevan – a luncheon in Pont Street – illness and resignation, 1947, 136

XVI Smoking Room politics – Jimmy Maxton and the Clydesiders – Liberals – Ernest Bevin – Press relations, 149

XVII Return to power – the Scottish Office – new Ministers – death of George VI, 160

XVIII A defeat – civil servants – the Forth Road Bridge – Bulganin and Khrushchev in Scotland – a farewell dinner – a misfire on the moors – Privy Council at Balmoral, 165

XIX Winston's retirement – Anthony Eden and Suez – a political heartbreak – reflections on Suez – resignation, 1957, 175

XX Last thoughts on Winston, 181

Index, 185

Illustrations

Between pages 42 and 43

The 1st Earl of Moray

Moray House, Edinburgh
The monogram on Moray House

Moray Place, Edinburgh
A modern view of Edinburgh

The author in 1910
Leaving investiture at Buckingham Palace, 1918

Between pages 90 and 91

The author in Oklahoma, 1922
With his wife and eldest son, 1932
With Harold Macmillan at Chatsworth, 1927

A sketch made by Winston Churchill to illustrate
his 'kangaroo scheme'

The author with Winston Churchill and Lord
Salisbury, 1936
With Neville Chamberlain, 1937

Foreword
by Sir Alec Douglas-Home

To write a foreword to James Stuart's book is an agreeable task because I can prophesy with complete confidence that its readers will never know a dull moment. Not only will they be vastly entertained by the many personal reminiscences vividly illustrated by very apt and funny stories but they will profit from the comments on many-sided life by a shrewd and acute observer.

The author has not attempted a serious political history, but for thirty years and more he knew many of the leading figures and every sketch of character and personality is authentic.

Very early on, at the age of nineteen, his colonel detected his ability to handle men and made him adjutant of his battalion which was fighting in France. This quality was often to be called in aid. Notably when he was summoned to be Chief Whip of the Government Party, years later, and finally, at the climax of his career, when he was that and much more to Sir Winston Churchill.

It is almost irreverent to suggest that anyone could 'handle' Churchill, but Stuart had a technique which was all his own. Here is a short extract following a proposal by the Prime Minister to appoint a certain person to office.

P.M.: 'Stop. You're not going, are you?'
Stuart: 'No. I'm only going to vomit. I'll be back in a minute.'
P.M.: 'Oh, so you don't like this?'
Stuart: 'Not much.'

He admits that Churchill was difficult and exacting to work for, but gradually a strong devotion grew to this 'generous', 'great', and 'remarkable' man, a devotion which the reader will see brought an intimate relationship of mutual understanding and affection.

But that is to anticipate, for the book opens with the author at war. Here are the realities of battle earthily told. 'The smell of a dead horse so much worse than that of a man.' The honour, glory, loyalty, comradeship, and then the squalor, waste, and tragedy – he shared it all. There is the sensitive, sympathetic, pathetic commentary on the hell of conventional war: 'As soon as a man's nerve gives way, he is liable to die quite soon.' And then a footnote to history in a reminder that the Germans were considered to be the 'top soldiers' and yet they never made a 'clean break or turned a flank', and Ludendorff was compelled to write that 'Haig remained master of the field.' And finally the verdict: 'All wars last too long. They waste too much of a nation's best blood, dissipate the national wealth and resources and achieve nothing useful at the end of the agony.'

But side by side with tragedy is humour and the ability to laugh, and every chapter is a mixed grill of gaiety and wit. Joe, the Oklahoma oil driller, chewing his tobacco while the author slithered on a four-feet greasy open platform seventy feet above him; Dick Molyneux, one of the last of the true eccentrics; Maxton the Clydesider, the lazy revolutionary, telling smoking-room stories unfit for the public ear; King George V's comment – 'Is it muddy outside?' – on the Prince of Wales's adoption of 'turn-up' trousers; an incomparable *Ode to a Seagull* by A. P. Herbert, happily preserved for posterity although at the time rejected by *Punch*; all this and much more, and the reader will find himself committing the unforgivable sin of constantly laughing out loud.

But finally we come back to politics, back to Churchill. (Although his nurse would have disapproved, he has kept the best to the last.) On the run in there are some significant asides about the famous: Baldwin, normally ticking over at half-speed, 'but capable of revving-up' and bringing into play great reserves of energy; Churchill's spontaneous tribute to the qualities of Neville Chamberlain, 'But what shall I do without poor Neville? I was relying on him to look after the Home Front for me.' And lastly that pithy sentence which marks his difference with Sir Anthony Eden over Suez: 'I didn't object to going in but to coming out.'

The years with Churchill are rightly the climax of the author's public life and of the book. It is a picture which is totally human. He describes it as 'fair and frank' and the reader will agree that it never oversteps those bounds. He does not skip or minimise the moments of disagreement, and yet every line is full of tolerance, understanding, and genuine admiration. The relationship between the two was that of respect, trust, and loyalty. They may be old-fashioned virtues but they serve the honour and dignity of man.

To many, James Stuart was an enigma. His friends who knew him well understood, but his political enemies could never get the measure of him. Of the host of stories about him the most apt is of the occasion when, as Secretary of State for Scotland, he was speaking inaudibly in the House of Commons and there were shouts from the Socialist Opposition to 'speak up'. 'Oh certainly,' he said, 'but I didn't know anyone was interested.'

On the first day of my association with him in the Scottish Office, he said to me, 'I think we ought to put a notice over our connecting doors.' I said, 'All right, what shall it be?' He answered, 'We will not overwork.' I was not deceived.

In this book he is modest about his achievements at the Scottish Office, as he is about his war service. But the reader will not be deceived either, for he will recognise that this is a life which has been spent in duty to the nation, and he will be grateful that there are still some who are not ashamed to serve.

'. . . In so far as I have risen to any position in this world it has been thanks to Sir Winston Churchill, because I served him as Government Chief Whip and also in the Opposition; then from 1951 until he retired as Prime Minister I had the honour of serving in his Cabinet. If it had not been for the pressure which he himself exerted upon me – and I say this in all honesty – I should have never entered his Cabinet. I had not contemplated doing any such thing: I had retired as Chief Whip some two or three years previously. But let me make it quite clear that I, at least, have no regrets. It was the most interesting, I may say absorbing, time of my whole life. He taught me more than anybody else has ever taught me. Indeed, when people have discussed education I have often said that my education began in 1940 when I joined Sir Winston Churchill. It may have been rather a delayed start, but there is a good deal of truth in it.'

Viscount Stuart of Findhorn
(An extract from *Hansard*,
25 January 1965.)

❦ I ❧

I think I have been lucky. I know that for the most part I have been happy, and I have no regrets. For why?—as the metrical psalms of Scotland ask. The answer is simply that I have been fortunate enough to be busy with things I have—again, for the most part—enjoyed; I have been closely concerned with interesting people and with events which already have their place in history.

For myself, I have not been driven by ambition, which can break a man's health or sour his disposition or go to his head. I have also been married for forty-two years to a wife who has put up with me and with the tiresome vagaries and relative impecuniosity of a life spent in politics.

Ambition has not always been entirely lacking in me, but it has been limited. I wanted very much to be adjutant of my battalion of the Royal Scots, and I achieved it before my twentieth birthday. When to my surprise I became a Member of Parliament and then—greater surprise!—a Party Whip, I developed an ambition to be Chief Whip. I held that office in my Party for eight years, in and out of government.

As a Scotsman who loves and cares deeply for the welfare of his country I was proud to be Secretary of State for Scotland for nearly six years, but that had never been a specific ambition, any more than I had ever anticipated working closely with Winston Churchill for more than a decade, in war and peace. These experiences were simply my good fortune.

So it cannot be said I ever reached for the stars. I have taken things as they came, and chance has played a big part in my life. I never sought power or the limelight, but chance led me to positions within the fringe of the area where power lies—the government of the country.

Yet I did not set out with political ambitions; I would have declined the initial invitation to stand for Parliament had not my

I

father said, 'Have a shot.' Thus, astonishingly, I won a seat that had been a Liberal stronghold for twenty-five years and remained the Member for Moray and Nairn for nearly thirty-six years.

Stanley Baldwin started me on the political ladder; Neville Chamberlain made me Deputy Chief Whip and a Privy Councillor; Winston Churchill made me his Chief Whip and then a member of his Cabinet. He 'made' me, taught me almost everything I know. He trusted me not to let him down, but neither of us had any illusion that I was a political genius.

Eventually I resigned office of my own free will because I disagreed, in the most vigorous terms, with my Prime Minister (Anthony Eden).

The origin of my family, and hence myself, can be stated very briefly, but I think is of sufficient interest to deserve a paragraph or two. Royal bastardy has played a big part in history.

King James V of Scotland was succeeded by his daughter, who became Mary Queen of Scots. To quote an authority on the Stuart family (H. M. Vaughan, author of *The Last of the Stuarts*), James 'showed great vigour and independence'. Among other things, he defied his English uncle, Henry VIII, refused to marry his daughter Mary (later known as 'Bloody Mary') and chose instead a daughter of the King of France. This unfortunate lady died six months later, but within the year James, aged only twenty-four, married another Frenchwoman, Marie de Guise, daughter of the Duc de Guise. They had two sons who died in infancy and after five years their daughter Mary was born. When the news was brought to James he said, 'It cam' wi' a lass and it'll gang wi' a lass'—meaning the Crown, which had come to the Stuarts 200 years earlier through a daughter of King Robert the Bruce. James V died a few days later and the historian Vaughan has written, 'His successor was his only legitimate child Mary. He left several bastards, among them James Stuart, Earl of Moray (the Regent Moray).'

The significance of this brief excursion into sixteenth-century history is that this 1st Earl of Moray was the progenitor of my family. He is an ancestor to be proud of, called by some 'the good Lord James' and by others 'the bastard Earl'. I derived considerable pleasure from Dame Edith Sitwell's book *The*

Queens and the Hive (1962) and found her writing: 'Although Mary was Queen, it was that most remarkable man, James Stuart, her elder half-brother, who was in all but name the ruler of Scotland'; and a few lines later: 'It was his misfortune and Scotland's that he was not King.'

We can now move on quickly to the 17th Earl of Moray, who had three sons, of which I was the third, born in Edinburgh in February 1897.

When I was four my father inherited property in Angus and Perthshire and we moved to the country. Just before my ninth birthday I was sent off to a preparatory school in Dorset and from there I followed my eldest brother, Francis, to Eton in January 1910.

I was said to have done poorly at my Common Entrance examination but I had my first 'little bit of luck' when at the end of my first half my sensible form-master, the late George Lyttelton, saw to it that I got a 'double remove' although I was absent with measles. By the summer of 1914 I had reached the Sixth Form, but although my name appears in the school list it is followed by the letters 'ABS' because I had joined the Army. So I missed my last year at Eton and the whole of the time I should have spent as my father intended at Trinity, Cambridge.

My getting into the Army was without parental consent. My father, a stern man, ordered me to return to Eton but I won my first battle with him by explaining that I had orders to join the Royal Scots at Weymouth on 15 September and that I would be court-martialled if I failed to report. It is unlikely that this would have happened, as I was five months under age for the Army anyhow. My father had grounds for annoyance. I had been disobedient, and also no doubt he felt entitled to discourage me from courting an early death. It is also possible that, since no notice had been given to the school authorities of my premature departure from Eton, he was annoyed at having to pay school fees for an absent son.

The First World War dragged on in tragedy and misery for four years and four months; like the Second World War, which lasted even longer but with fewer casualties, it went on far too long, which is true of all wars to my knowledge. What, for example, does anyone believe the Crimean War accomplished? Or the South African War? I doubt whether Waterloo achieved much after the French fleet had withdrawn in 1805 at Trafalgar and left us in undisputed command of a few acres of cold, wet sea. Trafalgar did put a stop to any further idea of the invasion of England, but Napoleon had already given that up two years earlier when he left the coast near Boulogne and ordered his armies to undertake that inglorious and in the end horrible walk to Moscow and back.

When the ultimatum to Germany was delivered in 1914 to the German Ambassador at No. 10 Carlton Gardens I was happily in camp with the Officers' Training Corps at Tidworth as a full private—the lowest of the low. I admit I had displayed no military zeal, but it was difficult to avoid joining the 'dog-potters', as we were called, if one was fit. The tragedy of my military life at Eton is contained in my mathematics master's report at the end of the summer half of 1914. The Rev. J. C. Chute, who commanded our company, wrote of me—and I still have his report—after commenting on my apparent lack of interest in maths, 'But what is more important than Stuart's mathematics is the fact that he will be Head of his House next half and he is so inefficient that I cannot possibly make him a lance-corporal in the Corps.' Too bad—yet a year later I was disguised as a temporary captain who had been in France with a regular battalion of the Royal Scots!

Luckily my father always held a low opinion of most school-masters, paid little attention to their reports and gave me mine to read and keep for my own amusement. Once, when I had got into bad trouble and was given as a *poena*, or punishment, '100 Greek lines daily with breathings and accents till further notice' (a severe punishment which lasted for ten days), he asked me what mis-demeanour I had committed. I told him, admitting that I and two others had broken a rule. 'Is that the whole truth?' he asked. I assured him it was. His sole comment was, 'Your housemaster must be a fool', and he never mentioned the subject again.

When the Foreign Secretary, Sir Edward Grey, coined his famous phrase 'the lamps are going out all over Europe...' we schoolboys in our camp were cheerfully unconcerned with these gloomy prognostications and satisfied that, for our younger world, the lights were just being lit up, and that as soon as we could get away from camp *we* would get 'lit up' too. This we did in a mild way when we reached London, but I was too young at seventeen and a half years to indulge in or to want strong liquor.

Tim Nugent (now Lord Nugent) and I got back to Eton and collected our civilian clothes. We had a meal alone together at the Bridge House Hotel and thereafter we got to London (where I lingered, before going on to Scotland) and discussed which regiment we should enlist in.

I remember Tim and I ended up in the old Monico at Piccadilly Circus where there were some Frenchmen and where we all got very excited, shaking hands madly and assuring one another that, together with the glorious French army, we would walk through the Germans in no time. There appeared to be no doubt that Berlin and victory could not take more than six weeks and our sole problem was how to get out there before the victory was complete.

When the band struck up the 'Marseillaise' we all stood up and shook hands again. Then a British party started to sing 'It's a long way to Tipperary' and we all had to stand up again and clasp hands because the French thought it was our National Anthem. (Similar displays of mutual esteem and affection embarrassed me in Rouen in January and February 1915, when British troops marched past the cafés to the exhilarating tune of 'Tipperary'; but by then, sad to say, we had begun to realise that the walk to Berlin was not yet far advanced in spite of the passage of six months instead of six weeks.)

But in September 1914 the mood was confident. Men of all ages had rushed to join up in any branch of the Services that would take them; many who could have been better employed enlisted as private soldiers rather than miss the chance of getting to the Front quickly. How many who feared that the war might end before they had got there lost their lives in the next few months?

The general feeling, quite different from that of 1939, was that we, with the French and the Russian 'steamroller' on our side, could not fail to achieve victory in a matter of weeks; 'over by Christmas' was the popular prediction.

Lord Kitchener was at the War Office, a great and popular figure, enjoying the reputation he had built up over the years as a successful soldier in many parts of the world, completely trusted by the public and regarded, in a way, as being 'above' politics. There would have been a tremendous public outcry if the politicians had got rid of him as any normal political Secretary of State might be disposed of today.

We all read his poster inviting us to join up 'for three years or the duration of the war'. There was no conscription or National Service then, and I am sure none of the legion of eager volunteers ever thought that 'the duration' might exceed the three years. They were caught either way.

I duly joined my battalion of the Royal Scots at Weymouth on 15 September and was happy to find a number of good friends from both Scotland and Eton among my comrades. We were under canvas on the cricket field and it was a healthy and happy enough life, with physical training, drilling, route-marching twelve or fourteen miles round Portland Bill to harden the feet, and occasional off-duty evenings in Weymouth.

It was a sketchy sort of training but it was all we got and all there was time for. Drafts of officers and men were being regularly dispatched to France from Southampton with little training and nothing that could be called knowledge of the military arts. What awaited them was the dull routine of trench warfare, which occupied most of the winter months, consisting of going into and out of the line for periods of four to eight days, depending on the weather and the condition of the trenches; throughout most of Belgium the mud rose above the boots and made it impossible to leave men in the front line for more than two to four days.

The continuing wet and cold caused 'trench feet' or frostbite. This affected in particular the 27th, 28th and 29th British divisions, regular soldiers who had been sent out on their return from India without being given time to acclimatise themselves. They went sick in hundreds. It was very sad, for these divisions were the flower of our Army—all long-service men and the most highly trained we had.

I was sent to France in January 1915 to join our 1st battalion, which had recently arrived from India with the 27th division, and one of the few things in my life I admit being rather proud of is that I got into the front line (near Dickebusch in Belgium) a few days before my eighteenth birthday in February 1915.

But during that first winter I was one of the many who had to go on the sick list; probably I had not yet acquired sufficient physical toughness to stand up to such conditions. I was in hospital before long and was invalided home in March.

When I was fit again I rejoined the regiment at our depot at Glencorse Barracks, near Edinburgh, and it was April 1916 before I went abroad again, this time to join our 2nd battalion, with which I remained—as happily as possible in the circumstances —for the rest of the war.

I found the battalion occupying precisely the same part of the line as I had been in just over a year earlier. Winter routine again prevailed and though the line was reasonably quiet apart from the usual intermittent gun and rifle fire the most disturbing feature of life was the trench mortar fire which occurred periodically each day or night.

In daylight one could see the big rum-jars, as they were called, coming through the air, lobbed at us from the German front line not more than 200 yards away. With good judgment it was possible to run round the next traverse in the trench, to right or left, before the explosion occurred, and we became very practised in this art. But I had a company sergeant-major (an Aberdeen police sergeant), a big, strong man who had developed a remarkable degree of fatalism—so much so that some of the men really believed he possessed some supernatural quality. He would sit down on an ammunition box in the trench, with his back against the parapet, and read a book during the mortar bombardments, and the men would sit down as near to him as possible and not even bother to look up to see the approaching danger.

7

There was, of course, a lot of good sense in his behaviour because any fragments from a shell that fell short would fly over his head which was below ground level. The danger was from a direct hit in the trench, but this was the exception and the law of averages was on his side.

Life pursued its normal course—four days in the front line, four days in the support lines and then eight days, all being well, in the brigade reserve about four miles back. Occasional raids were carried out by both sides, either with the object of scuppering some dangerous machine-gun or sniper's post or to obtain a few prisoners for identification purposes, High Command being anxious to learn which German division opposed various parts of our line and where their 'storm troops'—or crack divisions—were located. These raids usually caused some casualties and we also suffered (apart from the mortars) from machine-gun and rifle fire getting on to our wiring parties at night.

Wiring in front of the front line, say thirty to fifty yards out, was not a pleasant task and was cursed by all, especially on a bright moonlight night with the enemy about a hundred yards away and Very lights going up at regular intervals. Everybody felt like sitting, or standing, targets. Enemy patrols also might run into our wiring party and then anything might happen; it was a toss-up as to who got home safely.

On the return of a wiring party the dismal call for stretcher-bearers would be passed along the trench. I never heard a stretcher-bearer complain apart from uttering a prolonged stream of forceful oaths, mainly composed of a famous four-letter word used as noun, adjective and verb, and always aimed at the 'Jerries'. Stretcher-bearers, being unarmed, did not attack each other even if they happened to collide in No-Man's-Land, but there was always a danger of a wound or death by the bullet of a sniper or a burst of machine-gun fire. Somehow or other they always seemed to return with their stretcher cases, their return to our line heralded by the same stream of language that had attended their courageous departure.

In the trenches we all cheered up when the spring brought better weather; but not for long. I always said this life in France and Belgium was a choice between grave discomfort and some danger during the winter or better weather and excessive danger in summer.

Soon the rumours began and tension grew. The old soldier, perhaps of some months' standing, could be heard as he sat on the fire-step educating the new entry recently out from home as to what was coming to him soon in the way of real soldiering. Would we be sent a little north to 'that — Wypers', or would it be south to some almost equally abhorred part of the battlefields? The soothsayers were always right in one respect: we were always sent somewhere.

In due course our time came and we marched southwards keeping some miles to the rear of our line. Eventually there could be no more doubt and it was agreed amongst our experts in the ranks that the Somme was to be our destination.

I always enjoyed these movements behind the line. We marched, anything from ten to fourteen miles a day, which may not sound a lot, but if you are weighed down by a rifle, ammunition, pack, haversack, full water-bottle and entrenching tool it is not possible to move very far or rapidly in a day, especially as men were apt to 'fall out' owing to sore feet or other causes. The pace of the slowest prevailed, but to anyone who likes the country scene the French agricultural districts are truly beautiful in the springtime, and walking—or marching—is as good a way as any to see the countryside. The area abounds in orchards swathed in perfect blossom while the little villages and their churches are full of charm. I must admit that in 1916 there were also some unpleasant odours. I hope the modern visitor will find that sanitation has been improved in the intervening fifty years.

We halted and were billeted at the end of each day's march in some small village or farm where one could sit out in the evening enjoying the scent from the blossom; and we then slept in our 'fleabags' on the floor of the kitchen while the pigs grunted and snuffled around for food outside with the chickens, round the midden (or large sunken manure heap) which provided the life-blood of the farm and whose pungent though wholesome odours drifted towards our sleeping quarters.

Steadily and in accordance with the timetable of the General Staff we approached the rearward area of the great battlefield of the Somme. The initial attack had been launched on 1 July, but it had failed to break through or reach its ultimate objective. Some progress, however, had been made in our area and the first main

9

objective of the enemy's front line had been captured. They now held a strong support line, well built and heavily wired as was the German custom. Our task was to be the capture of the line in the first place and thereafter to build ramps to let our cavalry pass through, this being the dream of the cavalry generals who still occupied many high commands in this predominantly infantry war.

Sir Douglas Haig, the commander-in-chief, was himself a cavalryman; once again a return to open warfare was envisaged, with the cavalry charging gallantly (and hopelessly) against barbed wire and German machine-guns, and this type of outmoded warfare was to be advocated for many months and years to come.

On the way up to the Front one could feel a change in the mood of all involved. The pipers played us proudly through the villages and cheered us up a lot, for who can entirely resist the stirring effect of pipe-marches such as 'The Road to the Isles'? But cheerful men, who would normally sing or play the mouth-organ, became quiet and more thoughtful as we began to encounter ambulances with their wounded cargoes on their way back to the casualty clearing stations; weary and dirty troops moving back from the actual battle-front and prisoners of war on their way to the prisoners' cages. Of course, it was good to see how many of the enemy had been taken prisoner, but the captives were so dirty and bedraggled that they failed to raise our spirits.

We were part of a mass of troops pouring into a shallow valley out of sight of the enemy except from the air, but obviously the German airmen had reported back that thousands of troops were assembling. This concentration area was called—a typical army euphemism—'Happy Valley'. There was no shelter of any kind and we lived in the open or in occasional shell holes and scrapings of embryonic trenches.

After a couple of days messing about here we were ordered up by night to take over a sector of the new front line—an old German trench close to a ruined village called Louverval and facing High Wood, where there was much severe fighting later.

Our trench was not a bad one, but naturally, having been the enemy's, it faced the wrong way for us, and its field of fire was so sited. We relieved some friendly Australians who had survived the first assault and I was not greatly encouraged by one officer who told me how ghastly it all was and that the only thing for which he was grateful was that when he came out to France he had left no money in the bank back home.

The following day, 11 July, we moved out into No-Man's-Land to avoid the gunfire by being in front of the line, which the Germans naturally shelled. This was a clever enough move, but I have often wondered what would have happened if the Germans had sent out some strong patrols and found us. Probably they were disorganised or carrying out reliefs. Anyhow they did not do so and when zero hour came at dawn next day I do not think the Royal Scots had suffered a single casualty.

The frontal attack on the German line was allotted to two other battalions of our brigade, while we, in support and not immediately involved although in front of those who were to attack, dug ourselves in about half-way between the two front lines, at the bottom of a slight dip to ensure that the enemy fired over our heads. I have never seen men dig more energetically, for obvious reasons, and every man was out of sight in these new slit trenches before dawn broke.

The next stage was tragic and the attackers suffered frightfully. Held up by two rows of wire, each about ten yards deep and uncut by our artillery fire, they could not possibly reach the German line. They were under direct enemy fire at about thirty yards' range, and there we saw their corpses later.

The brigade on our left had been more fortunate and had captured their objective. It now fell to us to take the initiative and I was appalled by the thought that we might be ordered to renew the frontal attack. But luckily our commanding officer, Colonel Dyson, was no fool. He ordered the battalion bombing officer to take his bombing squad and a few volunteers and move along to the left and up into the neighbouring brigade's line, from where he worked along towards his right again, in front of us, bombing over every traverse as he went. In this way the whole of our brigade front was taken by about twenty-five men and with very few casualties.

They brought back more than 200 prisoners, including a German regimental commander, a brave man who refused to surrender his revolver. The prisoners were marched back towards the cages while the German colonel was taken before Colonel Dyson who assured him that if he did not surrender himself and his revolver he would have him shot on the spot at once. This settled the argument and he departed alive to join the other prisoners.

Our adjutant had been killed and there were, of course, other casualties, but my company still lived intact, due to much good luck. The casualties of the two assaulting battalions were terrible.

I was now ordered to move my company up to take over the right of the brigade's line in a strongly built German support trench, but, of course, again facing the wrong way. On my left I had friends in the form of another company of Royal Scots. We threw out a few advance posts to give warning of any enemy activity and set to work to consolidate our new line by building some bits of fire-steps wherever a field of fire could be obtained.

In the evening a handsome regiment of Indian cavalry arrived and passed over my line. They were beautifully mounted and the chain armour covering their shoulders glittered in the sunlight. Not long after this there were intermittent bursts of German machine-gun fire out in front, followed in due course by the return of the horsemen to a dry ditch, about a hundred yards in front of my line, which provided some slight shelter; and that was the end of that cavalry charge and the last I saw of any cavalry on the Somme, except for a brief but memorable episode later that night.

About 2 a.m. the English officer commanding this crack Indian regiment found me at my company headquarters, which consisted of the first three steps of an uncompleted German dugout. (Here, still facing the wrong way so that the entrance was open to German shell-fire, I remained for the next few days.) The cavalry C.O. asked me to take over his line from him before dawn and was quite peeved when I explained that I could not oblige because my orders were to hold the line I was already occupying. He then asked me to go with him to view his line—an invitation which, although very tired, I was too polite to refuse. He apparently thought I would be attracted by his line when I saw it but, as I knew, there was no trench at all, merely a slight depression in which his dark-bearded men squatted, with their beautiful horses towering above them. Their chain-mail epaulettes now glinted in the moonlight even more attractively than in the sun. But I still had no intention of moving my position and said so, whereupon the cavalryman became quite desperate, explaining that he must be out of the place and get away back to water his horses before dawn. This merely reinforced my view that cavalry were not going to be of much help to us in the war, but as a very young captain I did not think it was my place to say so.

In the end the cavalryman asked me if I would sign a short statement which he would write out in his field-service notebook, agreeing to assume responsibility for his line. I hadn't the heart to refuse, and I knew it could make no difference anyhow. Either the Germans would counter-attack, and quite possibly take both our lines, or we would continue our advance.

I did, however, make my way to battalion headquarters to show the note to Colonel Dyson, who asked me what the hell I thought I was doing taking over more line for which we had not the men. I assured him that I had not done so really and explained that there seemed to be no other way to satisfy the man, who had now set off in the dark behind us with all the king's horses and all the king's men. Dyson laughed and I started the walk back to my company, an unpleasant walk because of the presence in the trench of badly-wounded Germans whom it had been impossible to evacuate up to now owing to the pressure on the stretcher-bearers handling our own wounded. I hated the sight of these unfortunate men, some of them in grave pain, strewn along their own old fire-step or lying in the trench.

I had to make this journey a number of times and on one occasion one of the bodies was not in its normal position, which I had come to know. I was terrified and imagined he would be just round the next traverse waiting to kill me, so I retraced my steps and told one of our men to bring a bomb or two and come with me. I told him to stand behind the traverse while I peeped round the corner and to be ready to heave a bomb if I said 'throw'. In fact the poor German had only moved round in order to do his own private business away from the step on which he had to sleep.

One night on patrol I ran across one of the Indian cavalrymen, a tall bearded Sikh, with his horse dead beside him and one or both of his legs broken. I could not move him, and I was patrolling alone. (This was contrary to orders but it saved trouble for the men and, frightening though it was, I tried even then to be a fatalist.) I told the Sikh I would come back soon with stretcher-bearers, which I did. But on my return I could not find him and, for some reason, he did not help by making some sort of sound to guide us. The

13

field was of uncut hay, which hid him. Perhaps he thought I was a German but, if so, it nearly cost him his life because I had almost given up the search when I bumped into him. He had been lying out for more than thirty hours when we got him in. I offered him a cheese sandwich, but he would not touch it, whether on religious grounds or not I do not know.

My success during those nights on solitary patrol was to capture and bring in single-handed one German prisoner. Like me, he was alone, and he was lost in No-Man's-Land; he seemed to be even more terrified than I was. I was unarmed, as usual, because I couldn't be bothered carrying arms and was sure the game would be up anyway if I met any of the enemy. However, this one came with me like a lamb and there was considerable rejoicing at company headquarters.

Some two or three days later I noticed my prisoner sitting in the sun outside the company signaller's shelter. I was astonished and asked what on earth he was doing still with us and why in heaven's name he had not yet been sent back to join the other prisoners in a cage. 'Oh,' I was told, 'Jerry's all right and quite happy. Look, sir, he smokes cigarettes.'

I asked what he ate, knowing that it could only be our rations. I got the answer, 'Oh, Jerry's all right, sir, he don't eat much, do you, Jerry?' Jerry not unnaturally smiled, but I ordered him to be sent away down at once. The British Tommy is truly a strange person. My men had found a new toy; or perhaps it was their early upbringing coming out and they were in a perfectly natural, friendly way loving their enemy as themselves. I found it inexplicably odd, while they were disappointed in me for banishing this new-found friend.

One night when I was in front visiting my forward posts I ventured into High Wood and, hearing no movement or voices, went on to the far side of the wood about 600 yards beyond our own front line. I was able to report back that the place could be had for the asking, but nothing was done and not long afterwards the Germans reoccupied it and fighting was still going on for its possession weeks later.

At length a brigade major arrived to tell me that his brigade was going to relieve us in two or three days and renew the attack from our lines. He insisted that he must reconnoitre the ground in front before his brigade came up, so that he would know the country in advance. A noble idea, but I warned him that he could not go far owing to machine-guns in the Louverval orchard. He insisted on being shown the way, so I took him down a sunken lane on which my right flank rested and in front of which one of my posts was stationed but only visited and relieved by night. I told him he could go no further and that if he tried he would almost certainly be killed. However, he again insisted and we parted company. Soon I heard the usual bursts of fire and he was never again seen alive. He was awarded a posthumous V.C.— but what did this and similar such acts achieve? Nothing but the waste of good life.

The 76th brigade came up and attacked according to plan but with only limited success. We moved back, but were sent in again immediately nearby and spent the next few days carrying out four minor attacks aimed at straightening and improving the line. They were horrible days of constant shelling, with a lot of casualties and little to show for them. When we were eventually pulled out I had done nineteen days in the front line without a wash or a tooth-clean—the shortage of water was acute—and with only two pairs of socks to change over at daily intervals. I am still liable to change my socks at any time of day; I think it is just for comfort but I suppose it still seems a luxury because, all those years ago, I was denied it.

When I arrived back at our transport lines I decided the only way ever to get clean again was to burn all my clothes and start life afresh. I was so thick with lice and covered with German flea-bites that our doctor painted me all over with iodine to stop the itching. 'Lucky but lousy' would describe me as I emerged from my first experience of the Somme.

It was not long before we were back again. We stayed in or near Happy Valley and reorganised the companies with fresh drafts from home. In addition one had the dismal task of compiling casualty lists and writing to the families of those killed. Then, within two or three days, we were ordered up again, a little to the south near the river itself, and informed that a great honour had been bestowed upon us: we were to attack, on about 4 August, side by side with the French Army, on the extreme right of the British, and we must make a show of it to impress our allies with our prowess and ardour. Apart from all this bunk, it was a case of 'theirs not to reason why . . .' and obviously we would do our best. The outcome of this attack was, however, surprisingly different from our expectations.

At dawn we advanced and secured our first objective without undue trouble or delay—*but there were no French!* They had not moved, and there we were with our right flank in the air. About 2 p.m.—*après le déjeuner* and some red wine—little driblets of three or four French could be observed moving forward in very short sharp bounds and chattering incessantly. Thus by about 4 p.m., or ten hours late, the French also had reached their objective and we were all very friendly and congratulatory. They had taken the precaution of waiting to see that we did our part successfully before launching their assault, which I thought very odd behaviour.

Almost the only good thing about life in the front line was that we were our own masters much of the time during those days of wrath; we never saw any of the generals or Staff, so no one knew if we did the wrong thing. A few more days with our allies ended our time in the actual Somme battlefield and we were moved away to do another equally unpleasant job at Serre, not far off, where we suffered a complete setback and heavy casualties again.

I am not writing history, but I cannot move on from the subject of the Somme without recording (especially for a generation to whom the facts of the First World War are, to say the least, dim) that on 1 July 1916 the British lost 19,000 killed and sustained 57,000 casualties, which is, I believe, the greatest loss suffered in a single day by any army in the whole of the 1914–18 war. The official record of military operations for 1916 states (I think in very mild terms) that 'the troops were tired almost to the limit of their endurance'. British losses for the whole of the Somme battle were given as 420,000; French, 194,000 and German, 465,000.

✐ III ✐

On coming out of the Somme I was made adjutant by Colonel Dyson and so achieved, at nineteen, my ambition to be adjutant of a regular battalion of my own regiment. I also received, a few weeks later, the Military Cross. This recognition gave me more than normal satisfaction: it gave me self-confidence. Having survived the battle of the Somme I felt for a long time that I could weather anything.

This valuable internal sense stayed with me for the next eighteen months and it was not until early 1918 that it began to weaken. I was by then too tired, and at the same time I began to feel that my luck in remaining alive and unwounded couldn't hold out much longer.

Colonel Dyson had gone sick and his successor, Major A. F. Lumsden, sent from our 1st battalion at Salonika where things were quiet, turned out to be as good a commanding officer as one could have wished for—efficient, good at handling men, very tough when required but forgiving to any man whose heart was in the job. But he and I had a serious row in the early stages of our partnership when I told him that he was sacrificing men's lives by ordering me to send out two signallers to mend a broken telephone line in daylight, adding that we would know soon enough if the Germans attacked. He insisted on my ordering the unfortunate signallers to go. Having done so I walked away along the trench to cool off and on my return found the two men taking off their equipment. I asked why they were still alive and one of them answered, 'As soon as you had gone the C.O. came and told us we needn't go.' So both Lummy and I won, but we could not speak to each other for two days. Thereafter we became the firmest of friends and remained so until he was killed as a brigadier in the 15th (Scottish) Division in June 1918.

After our severe hammering at Serre, on leaving the Somme,

we were ordered to attack again. Lummy told the G.O.C. of the division (Major-General Cyril Deverell) that it was hopeless, and he refused to obey. Deverell was, of course, furious, but the brigade major came up and gave his opinion in support of Lumsden, to our vast relief—for Lummy had risked his own future by defying the divisional commander.

On my return from a brief spell in hospital at Doullens we reverted to our winter routine of going in and out of the line every few days near Bapaume, with the usual monotonous routine of wiring and patrolling and occasional raids, but the battalion bombers pulled off one very successful raid without a casualty. The Germans had a strongpoint in front of their line and when our men attacked, the German sentry decided on discretion rather than valour and dived down the dugout steps to join his companions below. Thus there was no shooting to attract attention. A row ensued between our bombing officer and his sergeant as to which should have the privilege of going down the steps first. The officer asserted his authority and the sergeant followed on his heels. He ordered the enemy to come up and surrender, or else he would lob a few Mills bombs down. The result was that without a shot fired or a scratch to themselves they brought back forty-two German prisoners.

I nearly got shot, though, because in the excitement I foolishly picked up a German steel helmet and put it on—and it was only in the nick of time that I stopped one of our own sentries from shooting me.

In March 1917 we were pulled out of the line and sent back a few miles into Army Reserve to train for the next battle and to dig a new backward reserve line. This was a pleasant change and literally the last real rest we ever got before the end in 1918.

A few weeks later we moved into Arras and were billeted in partially ruined houses where there were still a few civilians, with children who had never known life without shellfire and who had never slept anywhere but in a cellar. There were also three or four battalions of Royal Scots ready for the same show, so we had friends to visit and be visited by, and we played bridge and awaited orders. This was the last time I ever saw the whole of my battalion in good form and spirits and anxious to 'have a crack at the Huns'.

Zero hour was dawn on the morning of 9 April and three nights in advance we were ordered into the caves of Arras to be out of sight. They were very old caves and safe enough, but we were without blankets or kit and the roof dripped, causing the floor to be slimy clay on which we walked or sat and slept, all equally uncomfortable.

We were in the first wave of the attack and we advanced successfully, for once without very heavy casualties, and waited to be ordered to go on or to be passed through. In fact we stayed where we were in the German trenches—and it began to snow. The 29th Division were then ordered to pass through us and attack the village of Monchy-le-Preux, situated on a hill ahead of us. It was also decided once again (and, of course, fruitlessly) to launch a cavalry attack. A cavalry brigade came up, looking very smart and beautiful in the bright sun with the snow on the ground. We were in a German observation post half a mile away, and we watched them assembling in mass formation, making a sitting target in the snow for the enemy gunners. Horses are terribly vulnerable and the men could do nothing but sit in shell holes holding on to their reins. The shelling soon started and the massacre was tragic to watch. Loose horses were galloping all over the place and wounded men were moving back if they could walk.

My C.O. (Lumsden), a keen horseman himself, told our men to collect one or two horses in order to mount himself better. He then called for a volunteer who could ride to take a message over to the cavalry brigadier. He wrote on a page of his notebook: 'Why don't you scatter?' Our provost sergeant volunteered and rode off. He returned with the answer: 'My orders are to form up in mass at . . .', giving a map reference. This faith of the higher command in cavalry was pitiful in its consequences. On this occasion there must have been about 300 dead horses on the ground—as well as many men—before they withdrew.

Shortly afterwards the weather improved and when in May it grew hot we had to wear gas masks against the stench whenever we passed those horses. Incidentally, for those who have never experienced it, the smell of a dead horse is the worst imaginable and, so far as I know, much worse than that of a human.

The 29th Division captured Monchy at some cost and we went up again to relieve them on 1 May, with orders to continue the attack two days later. We had only a limited success on this occasion, losing two company commanders in addition to other casualties.

The official casualties of the battle of Arras are given as: British, 142,000; German 85,000.

My C.O. had gone to take over the brigade and I was left with all the responsibility of the battalion. General Deverell was pleased with my contribution and came up to see me. He told me that he was personally putting me up for a D.S.O. It was unlike him to go too far but in this case he had done so, for I never got the D.S.O. and he felt he had let me down. He sent for me and showed me the recommendation, with the comment of the army commander added: 'I regard this officer as being too young to receive a D.S.O.' That settled that, but they gave me a bar to my M.C. and I didn't mind. I had other feelings about it later because several of my friends and contemporaries got D.S.O.s, but they were in the Brigade of Guards and the Guards were always regarded by the Regiments of the Line as spoilt darlings.

Soon after this the French General Nivelle's disastrous offensive took place, causing huge casualties among the French and resulting in serious mutinies. Nivelle was at once replaced as commander-in-chief by Marshal Pétain, who did a good but ruthless job in dealing with the mutineers.

Our next serious engagement came in July with the third battle of Ypres, which was fought mainly to relieve any danger of pressure on the French, who were now incapable of fighting again during 1917 as a result of the Nivelle fiasco.

The battle opened on 31 July 1917, and never in history can there have been so much mud and blood in a concentrated area in a comparatively short space of time. The weather could not have been worse; not only tanks but guns stuck or sank into the mud. I have been told, and I can believe it to be true, that there has never been such a concentration of artillery fire of all calibres. When we went out, our divisional field gunners stayed behind to cover the incoming battalions and were not relieved for weeks. Like me, they had the worst experience they ever had in the war. We had approximately fifty per cent casualties in forty-eight hours when we first attacked; we advanced some 400 yards under very heavy fire, and there we stuck.

We were ordered to attack again at dusk on the same day and did so, but unluckily the enemy had planned their counter-attack at precisely the same hour. Confusion and chaos followed on both sides and everybody got thoroughly muddled up. Such of us as there were at battalion headquarters were ordered to go and do our best 'to safeguard the honour of the regiment'. It was the only occasion in the whole war when I set off rather hoping that I would be hit and not caring what risks I took. Eventually we formed a line of sorts though not as far forward as we had been that same morning, and at the cost of two company commanders killed and many other casualties.

At this time I met two curious examples of premonition. A few hours before we moved up into our assembly positions on the first night a company commander called Berry came to me with a letter and a small parcel addressed to his mother in Edinburgh and asked me to get them home to her after the show was over. I asked why— and what was on his mind. He told me that he knew he would never come back. I said the usual things about not being silly and we all had the same chance, but he was adamant. He was dead within twenty minutes of zero hour.

The other case occurred the following day with a very pleasant young subaltern called Palmer. His company sergeant-major, Brennan, a first-class man who had been with me when I first went out in 1915, told me that he was out in front in a shell hole with Palmer, lying within twenty yards of the Germans. Palmer had been doing very well all day, until suddenly he undid his belt, took off his revolver and said, 'Here, Sergeant-Major, you have this. I won't want it any more.' Brennan asked what he meant and Palmer replied, 'I mean what I say. I am not going to live longer'— and within ten minutes he was dead.

It is curious that as soon as a man's nerve gives way he is liable to die quite soon, and he seems to know it.

We were passed through by the 9th Brigade, who did no better than we had done and suffered as did all who were engaged in this battle. Our attack had been aimed at a village called Zonnebeek, which, in fact, no longer existed!

The casualties during this brief but costly offensive are officially given as: British, 324,000; German, 202,000.

Having got out of this mess, we marched back a few miles to places we had known well before. But now the men were silent and depressed, without a whistle or a song between them. They had come through the worst experience they had ever known and lost a good many friends. It was unspeakably tragic, but at this point Lumsden displayed a streak of genius and proved his knowledge of men. Outside a village where we had been happy in days gone by he halted the remains of our battalion and piled arms. He then addressed the men, telling them to fall out for two hours in the village while he and the officers would watch the rifles. They were on their honour to be back in precisely two hours and any man absent would be in the guard room for a month or charged with desertion.

Every man was back at his place in two hours. We marched on the last few miles and aided by some beer the men were soon singing again and feeling much better. It was a miracle, and who dare say that beer is not good for a man?

We were next ordered back to Arras and the winter routine continued until March 1918 when the Germans launched their last great push. This final supreme effort was aimed at breaking the Allied line in front of Albert and Amiens. Clearly the Germans must have known that Ypres had tired the whole British Army and that the French had their own internal troubles. Haig, fearing a breakthrough to the Channel ports, had kept most of the available reserve troops in Belgium, behind Ypres, leaving General Gough's Fifth Army, adjoining the French a few miles beyond Albert, with a long line to hold and few reserves.

I was, thanks to another 'little bit of luck', on leave in London when the storm broke. On my way back I got to Amiens by rail and then asked a lorry driver to take me as far as Albert. He said we couldn't get that far since the Germans had entered Albert early that morning. I went back to the British town major's office for advice and was appointed without discussion second-in-command of a troop train carrying about 2,000 men. Our task was to make our way back to Étaples, where this conglomeration of men of various races, including Portuguese and Indians, was to be reorganised, the men re-posted to their various corps.

The men hated 'Eat-apples' (as they called Étaples) as heartily as I did, but we boarded the train. They were all tired and ready for rest but I had been on leave and had other ideas, so, having seen all on board, I got together with my new C.O. (a total stranger of some regiment I forget) and we agreed our plans. The idea was that he or I must alight at every stop to make sure than no one left the train; I said I would see to the night-watch, as I was comparatively fresh. He welcomed this allocation of duties and, having packed him in to sleep and seen our mixed force settled down, I walked up to the engine to ask our charioteer about *his* plans. His harangue in French made it half-clear to me that he would take us to Étaples. I learnt also that we would pass through Doullens en route. I knew there was a good officers' club there so I produced twenty francs—then less than £1—and the good man promised to stop for a couple of minutes at Doullens, where I got off the train at about 10 p.m. and walked to the club, leaving my unknown colonel with the rest of our Foreign Legion sleeping the sleep of the weary just. So far as I know, the second-in-command was the only deserter from the train before 'Eat-apples'.

I found a bed and got some sleep, and then made an early start up the line again to Amiens. (There was nothing virtuous about my early start; it was simply for the good reason that I was afraid the military police might catch up with me.)

I was happy to find my old friends of the 3rd Division within two or three miles of where I had left them. They had not been broken through, but had been forced to pull back to avoid the dangers of an open right flank until the Guards division arrived to make some sort of a line.

As soon as I could, I made my way somehow to divisional head-quarters where I knew the Staff and insisted that I must see at once the divisional commander, Major-General Deverell. I explained, without trying to hide anything, exactly what I had done, and why, as a result, I was two days late in reporting back from leave. He said at once: 'But you deserted your post when you left that train and you are guilty of desertion. Why did you do such a thing?' I replied that I couldn't bear the thought of Étaples and the horror of a base depot camp with about 2,000 disorganised men, all total strangers to me. 'The very idea was too boring,' I said, 'even though it might have been safer.'

Deverell was a tough, efficient and brave soldier who believed that the only line to follow in war was 'theirs not to reason why'.

But he thought about my unusual case for a while and at last gave his decision. 'Well, Stuart,' he said, 'as you deserted *towards* the enemy and not in the opposite direction I think it may be overlooked on this occasion.'

I returned to duty that same afternoon and heard no more. I think Deverell was secretly amused. He became a good friend later and was responsible for my being promoted to brigade major not long afterwards.

When I reached my battalion I found we were on the right flank of General Byng's 3rd Army, with our 5th Army, under General Gough, on our own right. The Germans nearly succeeded in their plan to drive through between Gough's army and the French, but the thrust weakened as it moved forward beyond its railhead. They did, however, capture Albert and get to within about six miles of Amiens and the main railway line from the coast to Paris, which carried all the British supplies from Calais and Boulogne. We on the 3rd Army's right flank had to fall back to conform with the retreat of the 5th Army. Every man, including cooks, grooms and bandsmen, was thrown into the battle. The casualties were heavy and many of the 5th Army were taken prisoners, but eventually the attack petered out and the last big German offensive came to an end. (General Gough was much criticised and after the Armistice he was the only army commander who was not given a peerage or other recognition, and I had every sympathy with him.)

I did not know it, but it was at this point, in April 1918, that the tide began to turn.

✣ IV ✣

Although the great German *putsch* at Albert failed it had practically split our Allied armies and therefore caused great alarm and consternation. The political leaders from London and Paris, together with the military 'top brass', held a conference at Doullens to consider urgently what should be done to prevent a repetition of such a catastrophe. Lloyd George and Haig were our principal representatives and the conclusion reached would probably be described today as 'closer integration'. While Haig and Pétain retained their respective commands, a generalissimo was to be superimposed. This assignment fell to Marshal Foch, a good man and a good soldier, with more life in him than Pétain and less on the defensive.

Obviously at the moment of his appointment Foch had no particular plan worked out but on interrogation he replied to all and sundry that his policy was '*Attaque, attaque, attaque.*'

My own, not necessarily correct, view is that Haig didn't much mind who was supreme commander or what his functions were so long as he and his British armies were permitted to get on with their job without undue interference. There is, however, no doubt that Haig distrusted all politicians and took it for granted that the French, whether soldiers or politicians, would leak any secret, which the enemy spies in Paris would pick up. (Indeed history repeats itself: for the same reason in the Second World War Winston Churchill and General Eisenhower agreed that they dare not tell the Free French the date of our intended invasion of their own country of France—for which, *inter alia*, General de Gaulle has never forgiven us!)

Soon after Foch's appearance on the scene Haig, without any notice to his generalissimo, carried out a small attack with a limited objective, which was a success. Foch was over at British H.Q. in no time and, I was told, in a highly indignant state, demanding why he had not been informed or consulted. He must have received the

25

answer which turneth away wrath—and I know he was tactfully entertained by the staff—for before he left he suggested that Haig should repeat a similar exercise elsewhere. But Haig said little, indicating that he would consider what might be possible. He had his own plans. Two days later, without warning anyone except of course the commanders on the spot, he successfully carried out a much bigger attack. Marshal Foch again arrived to see Haig, but, be it said to his credit, his immediate comment was '*très joli mouvement*'—or words to that effect, as my French is poor and I may be wrong.

Thus by August 1918 the British had taken over the offensive, first in front of Amiens to relieve the railway junction and then with attacks in several other sectors. In May I left the 3rd Division rather regretfully, but my feelings were not what they might have been, for although I had served throughout the war until now with the Royal Scots my friend Lumsden had gone off to command a brigade and I did not care for his successor. I was promoted to brigade major of the 15th Infantry Brigade in the 5th Division, commanded by a charming officer of the Coldstream Guards, John Ponsonby. He broke most of the rules and refused to take life too seriously, which was quite a pleasant change from General Deverell.

One night when we were out of the line General Ponsonby asked me to dinner. We had champagne and after dinner we played bridge and he said he hoped we wouldn't mind playing for five francs (about four shillings) a hundred—a lot to me who had been playing for sixpence a hundred in my regiment. He explained that if he played for lower stakes he was apt to gamble. As it was he gambled outrageously throughout.

I was told of him that in 1914 when he was out on patrol some German cavalry advanced to where he and his adjutant were. They swiftly disappeared into a ditch, but unluckily at that exact spot the Uhlans halted to dismount and relieve themselves. When the following evening Ponsonby's Coldstream battalion was due to attack it was thought fit that their C.O. should address them before they moved off. This he did in the following words of encouragement: 'Men of the Coldstream Guards, your commanding officer was pump-shipped on by a Bosch patrol last night. I ask you to avenge this crime.' This, of course, cheered everybody up considerably.

Before the end of August 1918, and throughout September and October, we had our share of attacking. At first, when told that we were to attack so soon after the great German onslaught, I thought our High Command must have gone mad; but soon, to my surprise and relief, I found that we were all steadily advancing, while enemy prisoners and aerial photographs confirmed that German morale was crumbling.

Thus, in brief, we continued, but not without much fighting and casualties. It was hard going and exhausting work, but by early November we were meeting with little opposition and for the last two days before the Armistice on November 11 I never saw a German nor heard a shot fired. They had mined all their dugouts, crossroads, and railway bridges, which meant that life was still dangerous, but we had lost touch with the enemy since we were unable to keep up with their retreat—and this was a most welcome relief to us all.

We had now come to the beginning of the end and—although in my low sphere this was not yet known—reconnaissance airmen were confirming that German morale and discipline were breaking down, for photographs showed that they were not burying their dead or digging new latrines behind their lines.

After the Armistice we suffered from terrible reaction. There we were, thousands of us, hanging about in a dreary, wet and partially ruined countryside with literally nothing to do and nowhere to go. We were right out in front of our supply columns and lorries could not get to us until the craters at all the crossroads were filled in or railways repaired.

Eventually three armies were pulled back to live at railhead or on the Channel coast, while one army—the Army of the Rhine—was ordered up to Cologne. We were sent forward to the Brussels area. I enjoyed our march when we got on the move at last and all the men cheered up. Like Robert Louis Stevenson, an army will always travel hopefully, but not because it is better to do so than to arrive; unlike Stevenson, the soldier hopes for something better at the next stop.

We took fourteen days to make the journey and were then billeted in the small town of Gembloux, about fifty kilometres from Brussels but on the railway so we could go into the city whenever we liked when off duty.

We arrived at Gembloux before New Year's Day, 1919, and we got into Brussels to celebrate it. I found a couple of pipers and took them into a smart restaurant and night club called 'The Merry Grill'. This caused quite a stir and certainly woke the place up.

We had a lot of fun in Brussels during the next four months and I grew to love the place. The small restaurants provided excellent food and Burgundy, but it was expensive and I soon found to my horror that in a few weeks I had spent all my war savings of four years. However, as Winston Churchill once remarked to me, 'What is money made for except to spend?' (I had been commiserating with him over the loss of a large sum of money in the American slump of 1929, and all he said was—'Yes, how much better if I had spent it.')

But to return to Brussels, 1919, our difficulty at this time was to find ways of keeping the men happy. They were soon bored, and when classes were started with a view to educational uplift no one took much interest. We also played a lot of football and hockey; but this was no way to fill in whole days.

While I was in Brussels the Prince of Wales (now the Duke of Windsor) came to stay with King Albert of the Belgians. He was accompanied by his brother Prince Albert (later Duke of York and eventually George VI). They were young—Prince Albert was about eighteen months older than myself—and they did not want to stay in the Palace all the time. They had come to take part in the Victory Parade and had brought a small staff. In attendance on Prince Albert was Louis Greig, who had been a naval surgeon at Osborne and Dartmouth when the prince was a cadet. My brother John had known him in the Navy, and so I had met him. (He was also something of a hero, for he had been Scotland's rugby captain when I was a small schoolboy.)

Thus a few of us used to organise small parties and dances at 'The Merry Grill' for the entertainment of the young princes. We had a great deal of fun and I got to know the princes quite well. What I did not know was that this meeting with Louis Greig, and hence with Prince Albert, was to prove a turning-point in my life.

∽ V ∾

Before pursuing the main line of my personal story it is, I think, worth adding a footnote on the First World War, which played such a momentous part in the lives of all of my generation and, on the evidence of one's own eyes and ears, has not been overshadowed by the more recent and more protracted horrors of the Second World War but still engages the interest of many to whom one would have thought it could be only a matter of ancient history.

I heard Winston Churchill argue more than once that the High Command of the First World War achieved nothing and never 'got going' in Belgium and France on the Western front where the great mass of manpower and guns faced each other throughout four years with nothing to show for it apart from vast casualties.

I did try to explain once or twice when we were alone that it was the Germans who were regarded as the top soldiers, and I ventured to ask what *they* had ever done. For example, *they* had never made a clean break, nor had they turned a flank. I added that the German chief of staff, Ludendorff, had written in his diary after the eventual collapse of the final German *putsch* at Albert and Amiens in March 1918: ' . . . and Haig remained master of the field.'

From that phrase came the title of Sir John Davidson's book. Davidson, a close friend of mine, was Haig's chief of operations under Sir Herbert Lawrence, then chief of staff. Davidson's regiment was the 60th Rifles, while Haig and Lawrence were cavalrymen, not always loved by the infantry; but in truth and in fairness I must add that never, even on the Somme, at Arras or at Ypres, did I hear a single word of criticism or complaint, from private soldier to general, aimed at Haig, and since he remained our commander-in-chief for some four years I have always regarded this as a truly remarkable tribute to a man who devoted his life to his duty. He would willingly have sacrificed his own life to save his men.

Haig, like Kitchener in South Africa or the Sudan, did not himself indulge in, or permit in others, any frivolities. No women were allowed anywhere, apart from the admirable professional nurses in casualty clearing stations close up to the line or in almost equal discomfort in the base hospitals.

During the first battle of Ypres (in which to my relief I did not participate) when he had thrown the last man of his reserves to the line, Haig rode alone up the Menin Road. There was nothing material he could achieve now in this battlefield; the conduct of the battle was in the hands of the commanding officers on the spot. But the gesture was far from useless. He was seen by many: word of this solo 'personal appearance' was passed along the lines, and it was not forgotten. He wished to let it be known that he was with his troops in body as well as spirit and that his own life, which he risked deliberately, was of little or no account.

It was said of him in these days that he had put himself into training at Aldershot six months before the war began. He was a Lowland Scot with a streak of the Puritan in his blood and he felt, I believe, that he had a role to play in this world which was not only to fight the Germans but to defeat them.

Davidson told me that Haig overheard him once at G.H.Q. mess at Montreuil saying, 'If one has to be stuck at G.H.Q. one might at least hope to get something worth eating.' Haig at once interrupted and, silencing the whole company, addressed Davidson down the table with these words: 'When you are at war you do not eat what you like; you eat what is good for you.' The surrounding generals neither applauded nor dared to answer.

Much later Davidson and I were in Parliament together and after he retired he came to live in my constituency. We discussed Haig and the war, and whether the third battle of Ypres should have been fought at all. After one serious discussion about the Somme and Ypres, where as a young infantry officer I was very lucky to survive, he was moved to say, 'Well, certainly the Gods can't love you.' An outsider might have thought this rather rude but he was merely inverting what had been said of so many of my generation—that those whom the Gods love die young—and I accepted it in the spirit in which it was intended.

Davidson hated G.H.Q. and Staff life, but as Haig would not release him he gave up the Army in 1919, never having commanded troops in the field and saying he would not do so even in peace-time.

He remarked one day that it was a pity he had not known me in those days of 1916–18 because he might have got me 'another medal or more'. I asked whether he meant a V.C., or what? He explained that our allies used to issue new sets of medals periodically—like stamps—and gave British G.H.Q. its ration for distribution. He told me that, for example, he had to leave Montreuil rather early one morning to drive to French G.H.Q. to see General Nivelle. Davidson had not finished his porridge in G.H.Q. mess when the chief French liaison officer bustled in and hung a *légion d'honneur* on him, kissed him on both cheeks and expressed suitable sentiments of affection and regard from one brave ally to another. Davidson then drove off to French G.H.Q. to meet General Nivelle who, to his horror, pinned another *légion d'honneur* on him, kissing him, etc. His business completed, he decided he had time to call on his old friend, Marshal Joffre—affectionately known throughout France as 'Papa' Joffre—who in semi-retirement had been made military governor of Paris. While they were chatting 'Papa' kept opening and shutting drawers in his table. Eventually he produced a pipe (of a kind which was called 'Papa Joffre' after him) and gave it to Davidson. But he also rang for and gave unintelligible instructions to an A.D.C. Davidson left soon afterwards but as he was about to go downstairs from the military governor's office, the A.D.C. came after him saying, '*Pardon, mon général*, but the *maréchal* wishes you to return.' He did so, and to his bewilderment Joffre, who had now found what he had really been looking for, pinned a new *légion d'honneur* on his chest and kissed him on both cheeks with some words about *fraternité, amitié*, etc.

Davidson had now been given three medals between breakfast and *le five o'clock*. On the way back he told his driver to stop in Doullens where they would get some food. He was taking a short walk round the small town when to his amazement he saw a *légion d'honneur* in a pawnbroker's shop. He bought it for his

31

daughter as a souvenir, and thus by 9 p.m. he had accumulated *four* high-class French medals.

Soon after Pétain had taken command of the French he found himself faced with a ghastly situation, doubtless well known now to readers of military history but of which we in the British Army knew little at the time. It was said that more than twenty French divisions were mutinying and that Pétain had felt obliged to have many officers and other ranks shot after trial by summary court martial in the field.

I believe I am correct in saying that it was this that caused Haig to fight the third battle of Ypres, because Pétain impressed upon him his inability to stop the Germans being in Paris within forty-eight hours if they attacked the French front and that the only hope was that we should attack to the north and keep pressure off the French. Haig asked Pétain if he had informed the French government of the position. Pétain, to his credit, is said to have replied, 'If I told the French government, the Germans would know in twenty-four hours and then they could be in Paris forty-eight hours later.'

The Vimy ridge had been mined and was ready to be blown up in front of General Plumer's Second Army. Our tanks were being shipped out in substantial numbers for the first time and, late in the year though it was, Haig decided to launch a major attack in front of that most hated and desolate Ypres. Alas, not only the Germans but the weather also were against us, and not for the first time. Coupled with this, an Irish deserter gave away the date of the attack to the Germans and chaos was added to the mud in which most of our new tanks were bogged down within half a mile.

Our Prime Minister, Lloyd George, and the Cabinet in London had not been informed and for this reason Lloyd George never forgave Haig, but it was Pétain who insisted that no one must be told. We suffered a severe reverse but we may well have saved the French line.

All wars last too long. They also waste too much of a nation's best blood, dissipate the national wealth and resources, and achieve nothing useful at the end of the agony. It saddens me that in the so-called 'piping times of peace' (or shall we say—thinking of the present situation—non-war?) we produce an unending stream of thugs, cut-throats and train robbers, and this is largely attributable to war. The youth of the country is trained in war to take human life and the war attitude towards human life does not end with the generation personally involved. If the fighting man does not lose his life he is liable to be badly wounded, whereupon he goes to hospital and is cared for, repaired and fattened up for a later series of bloody battles.

The normal soldier's prayer in France or Belgium in 1914–18 was to get a 'blighty'*—a wound serious enough to send him home but not so light as to keep him in France. Hence the popular song which the troops sang cheerfully and without rancour on the march:

> Take me back to dear old Blighty,
> Put me on the train for London Town.
> Take me over there, drop me anywhere,
> Liverpool, Leeds or Birmingham, well I don't care!
> I should love to see my best girl,
> Cuddling up again we soon should be;
> Whoa! Tiddley iddley ighty,
> Hurry me home to Blighty;
> Blighty is the place for me.

How odd that people at an advanced stage of civilisation should spend so many years of a century fighting each other. It is contrary to the teachings of religion, and I believe most people have a religious (or moral or ethical) core somewhere inside them. It is not pious or evangelistic or unrealistic to say there is good in everybody. I once asked a prominent judge what purpose it served to put a man on oath. He said, 'The criminal classes do not like to lie on oath.' I believe that this is true not only of criminals. When I asked the question I had in mind a now almost forgotten man called Profumo, because it interested me that while he had on his own admission

*'Blighty'—the First World War soldier's slang for home—was really much older than 1914; it originated among the British soldiers in India and was corrupted from the Urdu (originally Persian) word *vilayae*, meaning 'country'.

lied to the House of Commons he flinched from lying on oath. This supports my belief in the presence of inherent 'good'—a hard word to define though we all know what it means—within nearly all of us.

War is also a contradiction of the rule of law by which all civilised men are agreed we should live. Yet war can be unavoidable in certain circumstances, and these existed in the case of the two Great Wars of this century. We and the French had to defend ourselves; it is as simple as that. In 1914 it was against a Kaiser suffering from maniacal *folie de grandeur* and in 1939 against an even more dangerous lunatic called Hitler, suffering from most forms of mental disease.

I asked Sir Winston Churchill once why he had always been so ardent a Francophile. He replied at once, 'On account of the need of French manpower against Germany.' Hence, indeed, the *entente cordiale* of Edward VII's day.

The Italians were misled by Mussolini, who was in turn misled by his own *tête montée* (to polish off the last of my French). He put them on the wrong, or losing, side in the Second World War, and for this suffered an appropriate if gruesome death at their hands. The Italian people did not suffer all that grievously for their tolerance of an intolerable leader, because they now seem to be prospering and possess a more than average number of millionaires. A prominent French general said of them in the First World War that it was a matter of opinion as to whether it paid best to have the Italian Army on your side or against you in the Line. His opinion was that while it cost three divisions to oppose them it would cost him five to keep them in the Line if they were on his side.

I recommend Eric Linklater's book *Private Angelo* to anyone wishing to read of the Italian soldier. While it is full of good entertainment, the reader is constantly worried that Angelo may find himself on the wrong—or losing—side at the end of his adventure; but luckily the end is a happy one.

There was an incidental side to the 1914–18 war which I would not like to overlook. There is light and shade in all things. London life was very bright and full of adventure to any youth during the war years. The theatres and music-halls boomed and there seemed to be more amusement then than there is today. It is a tragedy that the genuine music-hall seems now to have died out. Like Stanley Holloway, and unlike Rex Harrison, the performers of those days could sing full-bloodedly, and there were plenty of them. Revues or straight music-hall programmes abounded and one would arrive in time to see the turn one wanted. The songs were mostly patriotic, the tunes were tuneful, and the audiences were ready with enthusiastic applause.

Harry Lauder, an Ayrshire miner with, as my father said, a 'faultless true voice', was usually at the Tivoli in the Strand. Not only did he always fill the house but he always brought it down singlehanded. I still remember most of the songs which made him famous, like 'Stop yer tickling, Jock' and, of course, 'Keep right on to the end of the road'.

At the Palace Theatre in 1917 Miss Gwendolyn Brogden, who is an old friend and must be not far short of my own age, was singing:

> On Sunday I walk out with a soldier,
> On Monday I'm taken by a Tar,
> On Tuesday I'm out with a baby Boy Scout,
> On Wednesday a Hussar;
> On Thursday I gang oot wi' a Scottie,
> On Friday, the Captain of the crew,
> But on Saturday I'm willing,
> If you'll only take the shilling,
> To make a man of any one of you.

'The shilling' was, of course, the private soldier's daily rate of pay—quite a different thing from the private's twenty shillings-odd a day now!

Also at the Palace, Nelson Keyes, a curious dapper little man in immaculate tails and white tie, was parodying a patriotic song with:

> Red for the blood we are shedding
> Blue, though the skies be black:
> White, white—my country's never white,
> But there's always the Union Jack.

Basil Hallam, handsome and if possible even more immaculate, was the idol of the town with his 'Gilbert the Filbert':

I'm Gilbert the Filbert,
The Knut with a 'K',
The pride of Piccadilly, the blasé roué.
Oh, Hades! the ladies who leave their wooden huts
For Gilbert, the Filbert, the Colonel of the Knuts.

Or his other popular hit of the day:

None can say of me I'm not a constant lover;
Look how constantly I fall in love . . .

And so on to his last success:

Goodbye, girls, I'm through.
Each one of you I've met,
I say 'goodbye' to you
Without the least regret . . .

After that he left for France to serve as an observer until one day his observation balloon was shot down by a German pilot. Thus, like many others, he died gallantly.

When one had had ten days' leave in England (or in my case sometimes in Scotland) one returned feeling a lot better and infatuated with the many lovely actresses that there were. I knew none of these personally except Miss Zena Dare (Mrs Maurice Brett). She was in Paris for a time where her husband (of the Black Watch) was provost marshal. She was, and is, beautiful; I had known her since my Eton schooldays when she came to tea with me, bringing, to my regret, her father-in-law, Lord Esher. It was like the old music-hall song, 'And her mother came too'.

The next best thing to ten days' leave at home was three days' 'local leave' in Paris, where every prospect pleased and the French were all charming to us, welcoming us almost as heroes. I took Zena (and Maurice came too!) out to lunch in the Bois and they dined me and took me to a cinema. Once she let me drive her out to Versailles on a lovely afternoon, my first visit to that great monument of French civilisation; but I was far too shy of so beautiful a celebrity and I don't suppose I even opened my trap.

I know her much better now and have none of the trouble in conversation with her that I experienced at the age of twenty, or less; I even went on the stage to pay homage to her at Drury

Lane while she was in 'My Fair Lady' and was the subject of one of Mr Eamonn Andrews' 'This is your Life' television programmes. I confessed freely to all that vast viewing public that I had been in love with her since I was sixteen.

I was lucky enough to get three Paris leaves between 1916 and 1919, but the last one, in December 1918, was highly irregular. I was then a brigade major and my brigadier told me he was putting in for Paris leave and wouldn't I do likewise? The Armistice was behind us and there was no more war, but I had been too 'recently' on a whole month's English leave (in fact, it was nine months earlier) so my application was turned down. But the brigadier, having fought his war, was in a 'bonhomous' mood and said, 'You're not a regular soldier so you have little to lose. Why not risk it and come along?' I accepted this very improper suggestion from my superior, explaining that I knew the A.P.M. (Brett) and that I would report to him in Paris and tell him that his military police could always pick me up at the Hotel Meurice—if they must. They didn't, and so an enjoyable three days was had by all.

I feel that this brief interlude of reminiscences is justified to off-set the 'mud, blood, and tears' aspect of 1914–18, so far as possible. But it remains a fact that the life of those years was monotonous, largely a case of relieving each other at eight-day periods in summer or four days in winter. During battles or attacks—like the Somme, Arras or third battle of Ypres—one remained constantly in the line if one survived. My nineteen days on the Somme without a break in July 1916 and those seventeen days at Arras are not easily forgotten. I once wrote to my old nurse in Scotland that the war reminded me of one of those last verses in a chapter of the New Testament which reads, 'Jesus Christ, the same yesterday, and today, and for ever.' My mother wrote asking me to desist from any repetition of my misguided so-called humour.

But shortly afterwards, my nurse's answer arrived. She reproached me for getting my biblical reference wrong and said that I meant something as different as chalk from cheese. What I must have in mind, she said, was a verse from some other book of the Bible to the effect that only the 'silver vessels come through the furnace'. I hope that she had me in mind as a 'silver vessel' but I

can't be certain, any more than was that virgin from Kirriemuir in
the old rhyme which runs:

> There were fower and twenty virgin
> Wha' went oot frae Kirriemuir,
> But only one came back again
> And she was nae sae sure.

I was demobilised on returning to London and went up to Scotland to see my mother and father. It was my intention to give my family the pleasure of my company for a longish period as I thought I deserved a holiday and a rest—in spite of the fact that I had been idling around Brussels for three months. But I soon became restless and my mother clinched things one day by remarking, with studied casualness, that my father never liked to see any of us hanging about at home for more than three weeks at a time. It worried him to see us idle. So she advised that even if I had nothing in particular to do I should at least pretend to have some plan or occupation—in other words that I ought to remove myself for a time.

My mother was a wise woman and I always took her advice if it was possible to do so. I didn't know what to do—or invent—but the problem was soon solved when our family solicitor and good friend, Mr. H. E. Richardson, arrived on a visit. I am sure my mother briefed him in advance, for he proceeded to propose that I might read for the Bar, which meant that I would move to Edinburgh.

My career in law did not last very long and the Bar certainly lost nothing of great value when I moved elsewhere. Dutifully I walked up the Mound from Princes Street every morning at nine o'clock and listened to long lectures. I completed my course in Public International Law under Professor Sir Ludovic Grant, but my memories of the period are mainly frivolous.

The Professor was a charming man. He had a habit when lecturing of turning to a blackboard behind him whenever he came to a proper name or place-name and chalking it up boldly so that we would get it right in our notes. I remember our pleasure one day when, quoting the case of *Rex v. Smith*, he turned round and spelled out SMITH on the blackboard. But even with such careful aids to instruction my place in my classes was not good enough. I had good friends among my fellow students, some of whom I still know and who have gone on to dizzy heights, including the Bench, but I was not of their calibre and always seemed to finish half-way down the list, or worse.

I was worried about this, but that did not prevent my enjoying golf at Muirfield or elsewhere at the week-ends, and the social life of my native city. While reading law I was apprenticed to a well-known firm of Writers to the Signet—the splendid Scots title for solicitors—named Tods, Murray, and Jameson. Only influence can have persuaded them to take me under their wing to learn something of this side of the law. It was a highly respected and dignified firm, acting only for the best people. The late Lord Horne (Sir Robert Horne, K.C. and one-time Chancellor of the Exchequer) used to like to recite some lines to exemplify the snobbery of Edinburgh life in his time, which was somewhat earlier than mine. They went:

> It was luncheon time in Auld Reekie,
> In Jameson, Murray and Tod,
> And the Blackburns talked to the Pitmans,
> And the Pitmans talked only to God.*

Lord Blackburn, a well-known judge, had married a sister of the Earl of Strathmore (father of Queen Elizabeth the Queen Mother) while the Pitmans were one of the best-known families in the city.

I have always been rather embarrassed by reference to Edinburgh as the 'Athens of the North' but I am prepared to say that the Scottish capital and Bath are the two most beautiful cities in Britain. Robert Louis Stevenson† has written eloquently and informatively about the Old Town, lying around the Castle, on its majestic rock, with the Royal Mile running from it down the High Street and Canongate to the royal palace of Holyroodhouse; and of the New Town (which would be regarded as old in most cities) which was

---

*A parody of the American rhyme on Boston snobbery:
> Where the Lowells talk to the Cabots,
> And the Cabots talk only to God.

†R. L. Stevenson: *Edinburgh, Picturesque Notes* (1878).

laid out when times were thought to be more peaceful, and the city as a whole (defended against the North, be it noted, and not against the English) began to take shape. The 'Nor' Loch' was drained and became Princes Street gardens; after which the Mound was built, leading from the new Princes Street up to the Old High Street.

Sir Henry Raeburn, the artist, who lived and worked in Edinburgh, referred to the New Town while it was being built as 'the draughty parallelogram'. Not a bad description in some ways: for example, where the Waverley Steps ascend from the railway station to Princes Street the 'draught'—often more like a gale—coming round the west side of the North British Hotel can be so strong that railings had to be erected to prevent people from being blown off the pavement into the busy traffic of Princes Street.

My family had owned an Edinburgh house from its illegitimate start in the sixteenth century until my own father's day—Moray House, still standing in the Canongate; and when we left the Old Town (or Auld Reekie) my ancestor bought a house, then outside the city, called Drumsheugh House. The site is now called Randolph Crescent, after Randolph Earl of Moray. He was ahead of his time, because Raeburn's 'draughty' New Town came after him.

Lord Cockburn, the famous Scottish judge, refers in his 'Memorials' to the agreeable view of 'Lord Moray's pleasure grounds' to be seen from the west end of Queen Street, where at that time the new development ended its advance to the west. My family developed this later—after Charlotte Square, which is the most beautiful square in the new area. But our circular Ainslie Place and Moray Place are not bad, with their gardens in the centre and the pleasure grounds still running down to the Water of Leith, below the Dean Bridge.

The original plan for the New Town intended that Princes Street should be residential while George Street, parallel to it to the north, should be the shopping area. But the plans of planners are liable to go astray and during the past sixty years I have no recollection of seeing a single private house in Princes Street. It is all shops, but for an occasional club or hotel.

Edinburgh has many civilised virtues. It is possible to play golf on first-class courses in all directions between North Berwick and

41

the Forth Bridge. I will not enumerate them, but I have certainly played on ten within an hour's drive, and in my period of living there one could reach the Braid Hills course by boarding a corporation tramcar which deposited one at the gate within two miles of the west end of Princes Street. Also, and more surprisingly, it is possible to shoot grouse on the Pentlands, within ten miles of the centre of the city.

The tramcars have gone now, but they too were unlike anything I have seen elsewhere. The originals were drawn by a moving cable a foot below the level of the streets. There must have been miles of moving cable since one could travel down to Leith, up to the Braid Hills to the south, or westward out to Corstorphine; and there were no overhead rails or standards to interfere with the beautiful view of the dominating Castle.

Edinburgh and golf seem to me inseparable and I have always enjoyed an old story about the then new and impressive Waverley Station. Some golfing friends in St Andrews decided to give a trip to Edinburgh for the day as a sixtieth birthday present to an old friend, a caddie, who had never ventured so far afield as our capital city. They gave him a return ticket and a bit of pocket money for expenses. They also agreed that two or three of them would meet the last train back in case the birthday boy should have gone to sleep or be otherwise incapable of getting out at the right place. However, he arrived safely, if rather the worse for wear. But on being asked what he thought of the capital and if he had seen the sights, the caddie replied, 'Och, it's a gey queer place is Edinburgh; it's a' roofit in'. He had, of course, never left the station, under whose acres of glass roof there are numerous bars and refreshment rooms.

A decision on my part about my future in the law proved to be unnecessary. Suddenly, after I had been in Edinburgh about a year, my whole life changed. I was asked by Louis Greig to come to London to see him. Prince Albert had gone to Cambridge after the war and the suggestion was that I should join him there about a month before he came down and started his official career. I was to be his first Equerry. Such a thought had never entered my head, but I was given a little time to think. The pay was not big (£450 a

42

The 1st Earl of Moray (1531–1570).

Moray House, Edinburgh—the old home of the Earls of Moray in the Canongate.

This stone monogram on Moray House is often taken to stand for 'Moray House' but it in fact commemorates the marriage of the 4th Earl of Moray to a daughter of the 1st Earl of Home.

Moray Place, Edinburgh. An example of the 'New Town'—or early nineteenth century—architecture, and named after the Stuart family.

A modern view of Edinburgh, from Calton Hill looking west, showing the Castle (*top centre*). Princes Street (*right*) divides the Old Town (*left*) and the 'New' or Georgian Town.

The author in 1910. The occasion was the Fourth of June celebrations at Eton.
The author, as a captain in the Royal Scots, leaving the investiture at Buckingham
Palace in March 1918, when he received his Military Cross and bar.

year) but I would have my own bedroom in Buckingham Palace and would share a room to work in with Louis Greig. I would be given breakfast, and lunch any day I chose, and I could 'warn in' for dinner with the Equerry on duty to the King (George V) if and when I wished.

After some consultation at home I replied that I would accept but that I could not do the job for long because of the need to earn more. The answer to this was that it was not worth starting if I was going to walk out at any moment, so we settled for a period of not less than one year and not more than two. I stayed for eighteen months.

❦ VII ❧

Life in Court circles was an interesting experience and quite unlike anything I had known before—or indeed have known since. When I left Buckingham Palace and looked back on my eighteen months there it was almost impossible to believe it had really happened, especially as—to anticipate just a little for dramatic effect—my next job was in the oilfields of Oklahoma, where it was out of the question to mention where and how I had last been employed.

It was a comfortable life at the Palace; I mean one couldn't complain that the roof leaked or that one was ill-fed. But there was no ostentation and, apart from official banquets or Ascot Week at Windsor, the Court of George V went in for no excess in the way of food or drink.

Everyone was charming to me, although at twenty-four I was a good deal younger than the other members of the royal entourage. They helped me in any way they could and, looking back, I think I may even have helped them, or at least amused them, by bringing a breath of the outside world in such forms as the current stories from White's or the Bachelors' Club. Mostly they were out of touch with such things. They all belonged to the Marlborough Club more or less out of loyalty because Edward VII had started it. (I have been told that he was moved to do so because of some differences of opinion over smoking a cigar in a certain room at White's.) I avoided joining the Marlborough by pleading impecuniosity. A fair enough excuse, I think, but I had also satisfied myself that it was deadly dull.

Yet it was a somewhat lonely life at Buckingham Palace. My solitude was due to the fact that the Prince of Wales was established in St James's Palace with his own staff, which included Claud Hamilton, Godfrey Thomas as secretary and Bruce Ogilvy as Equerry. All three were and still are friends of mine and I saw as much of them as my duties permitted. I remember a somewhat riotous evening at the Café Royal and the Victoria Palace before Bruce's marriage.

My room in the Palace was on what was known as the school-room floor. It faced towards Admiralty Arch and, being high, had surely one of the finest views possible in London. The other inmates of the schoolroom floor were my boss, Prince Albert, Princess Mary (the late Princess Royal) and Prince Henry (the Duke of Gloucester). Prince George (the late Duke of Kent) was serving in the Navy and when on leave usually stayed with his eldest brother at St James's Palace. I think that as a young naval officer on leave he found more freedom there to come and go as he wished, and I certainly didn't blame him.

Now that I have myself taken part in the upbringing of a family—two sons and a daughter—I see more clearly, and regret even more, that George V did not have the knack of 'getting together' with his children. He was the most conscientious of men and I should think never faltered or failed in doing his duty to the smallest detail. He was absolutely honest and fair in all his dealings with officials and staff, and he was always charming with me. But then he bore no responsibility for me or my upbringing and could have simply sacked me any day he wished. (No trade union for courtiers!)

But in his relations with his children there remained something of the manner of a stern and caustic naval commander. I have a theory that this was at least partly because he spent longer in the Navy than he would have if he had been direct heir to the throne instead of the younger brother who succeeded because the elder died. Certainly he had clearcut views and he expressed them—with his wishes and criticisms—in no uncertain terms. He was well versed in the language of the gun-room and the ward-room, but the idea of dealing with children by such methods as discussion and persuasion was foreign to him, which I think was a pity.

The younger generation may be surprised to learn that a King (or King-to-be) of England was a lawn tennis player of Wimbledon standard. I find that many people have forgotten this unusual accomplishment of George VI when he was Duke of York. His prowess was due to the coaching of Louis Greig, who partnered him at Wimbledon in 1921. I believe they would have fared better but for Louis's over-anxiety that they should do well and that he should not let his royal partner down. As a result he tried to do too much himself and be in too many places at the same time.

I was a pupil of Louis's too, and, public engagements permitting, we used to play in the garden of the Palace. Louis partnered Princess Mary and I the Duke. Our bugbear—if it does not sound disrespectful to august bodies—was the frequency of such events as City of London banquets when the invitation was usually for some such maddening hour as '6.45 for 7.15 p.m.' Our tennis had to be curtailed and a hurried bath or shower at six o'clock was followed by a scramble into starched shirts—a sticky process—and hurried fumblings with dress studs, white ties and making sure that decorations were properly aligned. (I retain my opinion about the awkward timing of City dinners even though in later years I became Prime Warden of the Worshipful Company of Fishmongers.) I had to accept the fact that the uncivilised timetable was necessitated by people living outside London who needed adequate time to get through too many courses at dinner, listen to all-too-often tedious speeches, *and* catch the last train home clutching a presentation box of excellent chocolates to appease their waiting wives.

One afternoon our tennis was disrupted for a different reason. Louis Greig asked Princess Mary if she would be ready to play at 4.30, as we had to go out somewhere later. She said this was too early as she had to have tea with the King and Queen. Improperly, I suppose, we suggested that she might skip tea or that we could perhaps start playing at 5. But it was no good; she explained that she would have to change her shoes, which involved a longish walk from the Garden House (where tea was taken) to her bedroom. Louis then made the daring suggestion that she might go to tea in her tennis shoes, but H.R.H. quickly explained that the King would take a very poor view of any such behaviour. Our game did not take place, and I mention this only to give some idea of the strict code of behaviour upon which George V insisted even within the family. (The case of the Princess's shoes also recalls the occasion when the King first saw the Prince of Wales wearing trousers with turned-up bottoms and asked coldly if it was muddy outside.)

Another rule during my time at Buckingham Palace was that the

Equerry or secretary on duty had to discard his normal short jacket and put on a frock coat whenever the King rang for him.

I was particularly proud of my frock coat, which cost me about twenty guineas even in those days. I have always thought the frock coat much smarter than the so-called morning coat—the swallow-tailed conventional wedding wear nowadays—and I was delighted to sell my tail coat for three guineas to Moss Bros, which was at least a contribution to the high cost of my frock coat. Later a young naval officer friend of my brother came up to me one day and said: 'I'm wearing your tail-coat.' He had hired it from Moss Bros and it still had my name on it. He told me what he had paid and, remembering my three guineas, I realised that hiring dress clothes is a good business to be in. I later sold my frock coat privately for £5, but by that time I was lucky to find a buyer at all—a man who was just entering Court service.

My frock coat was a source of amusement to some of my friends when I was assigned to a tour of duty at Windsor during Ascot Week. They were amused to see me even as a courtier, let alone as a racegoer (which I have never been); but the frock coat was the last straw. Duty at Ascot led nevertheless to one of the most fortunate and important events of my life. I was watching the royal procession driving up the course one day when Lady Moyra Cavendish, indicating a certain carriage, said, 'Do you know my new niece, Rachel? She's staying at Windsor.' I said I did not, so she pointed out her niece and said something like, 'Doesn't she look nice? I must introduce you.'

What Lady Moyra meant by her 'new' niece was that the poor girl had just come back from Canada where her father (the Duke of Devonshire) had been Governor-General for the past five years and she had not lived in England since her schoolgirl days. She was now facing all the ghastly dangers of being a débutante and, as her mother was Mistress of the Robes to Queen Mary, she was being given a good start to her 'coming out' by being bidden to Windsor for Ascot. (Her elder sister, Dorothy, by the way, had married one of their father's A.D.C.s, a badly wounded young Guards officer named Harold Macmillan.)

I was duly introduced by Lady Moyra to her 'new' niece, Rachel, and I suppose her royal send-off into society may have been regarded by some as rather a flop, for she chose to marry me.

47

King George VI, previously Duke of York and still merely Prince Albert when I first joined him at Cambridge, was not an easy man to know or to handle, and I cannot pretend that I ever became a close friend; indeed I do not know of any very close friends he had, except Louis Greig, who had been with him for years during Osborne, Dartmouth and at sea in his first ship, where he became ill. They put him ashore at Rosyth and Louis escorted him to Edinburgh where he was operated on. He liked Louis and always said that he saved his life at that time.

Living for a time as close to him as I did—literally in neighbouring rooms—I got to know him quite well and we got along quite amicably. I hope I gave what was required of me. He was never a strong man physically and this doubtless affected his outlook on life. It was a great worry to him that he suffered from a serious stammer which affected him as soon as he started on a public speech. This is a terrible handicap to any speaker, but then ordinary people can generally avoid much public speaking. In his exalted position, however, it was a duty of which no one could relieve him. I was desperately sorry for him on those occasions and was always in a sweat of anxiety on his account. But I am afraid I was not then the right person to provide the sympathy and inject into him the self-confidence which was vital. In ordinary conversation he talked perfectly naturally, which proves that his impediment was a nervous affliction, born of shyness. But we had to pursue our normal round of public duties and it was not always easy. Later, of course, he took expert advice and improved enormously.

Apart from the more formal engagements there were the occasional visits in the country. Lady Leicester, grandmother of the present peer, was a charming lady but somewhat vague at times. I remember being in attendance when she was to receive H.R.H. for her opening of some flower show on our way to her home at Holkham in Norfolk. When we reached the local hall I said I would get out of the car to discover whether the audience was seated and the platform party ready.

As I entered, Lady Leicester, to my horror, rose and came forward to greet me, curtseying as she did so. The rest of the audience knew well that I was not the right man but they had not a clue as to who I was or why I was there. I murmured a few words of

apology and explanation, then hurrying from the hall I invited
H.R.H. to enter and receive the official welcome. I couldn't have
been more embarrassed but it is just such *contretemps* that
courtiers on duty have to try to be ready to cope with.

H.R.H. was a good shot and a good tennis player, but he didn't
like it when he failed to hit the ball well at golf. He had a quick
temper and golf did not suit his temperament. His outbreaks of
irritation, however, did not last, and his loud criticisms were
directed at his clubs. When I saw the Duke of Windsor for the
first time after the Abdication—ten years after the event and in New
York—one of his first questions was whether 'Bertie' still got angry
over golf. I answered that to my knowledge he no longer played
but concentrated on cutting down rhododendrons in Windsor
Park, which he probably found a more satisfying and less irritating
occupation.

I am not quite sure how to describe an Equerry, but he is a sort of
A.D.C. and glorified bell-hop. He usually comes from one of the
Services and wears uniform on day-time duty and Household
uniform when on duty at night. He used to wear knee breeches, as
I did, for evening parties, and the tail-coat had metal buttons,
similar to those of a footman, engraved with the Royal Arms.
This enabled one's host or hostess to get hold of the Equerry on
duty if ever the need should arise.

My two most miserable mistakes as an Equerry were unfortunate
at the time but not the end of the world. My master, then Duke of
York, had to meet and shake hands with the opposing teams of
the R.A.F. and the Navy at a cricket match. I told our driver,
Wood, to take us to Lord's. When we got there two men were
painting the gate and no one else was visible. I suggested that they
might climb down from their ladders and help open the gates so
that H.R.H.'s car could enter. We entered but there wasn't even
a cat in sight. The match was at the Oval! Horrified to have even
dented the royal reputation for punctuality, I telephoned saying we
had been delayed and that they should carry on, adding that
H.R.H. would meet them at the luncheon interval, which we did.

My second master-stroke of futility was when we had to dine
with the Archbishop of Canterbury at Lambeth Palace at 7.30 p.m.

to meet the 'Sons of the Clergy'. My London geography, beyond a certain limited area, was not at all good then and I told Wood, in advance, where we had to go, adding, 'It's somewhere across the river I believe—some palace called Lambeth.' We drove off and after crossing the river went on for some distance until H.R.H. said to me, 'Where on earth is Wood taking us? We must be miles away.' I did not know so I wound down the intervening glass division and asked. 'Well,' said Wood, 'I've found some sort of music-hall or cinema down Lambeth Walk and I suppose that's what you want.' There were indications of irritation from our royal employer but eventually we got going in the reverse direction, found the river again, and so the Palace, episcopal rather than theatrical. We were about twenty minutes late and I fear that many of the 'Sons of the Clergy' were getting hungry.

Among the courtiers around King George V I really knew Sir Reginald Seymour and Sir Sidney Greville best, but Sir Harry Stonor, like Sidney Greville a left-over from King Edward VII's days, was a character in his own right. He was tall and immaculately turned out: never a crease anywhere except up the *sides* of his trousers, following the King's custom; it was even said that Harry had his pyjamas ironed with the creases up the sides, instead of front and back, to keep the King company. Harry, like Sidney Greville, was a Groom-in-Waiting, being a little past the more exacting routine work of an Equerry, who did a month on at a time, day and night. I had no relief because I couldn't afford to share my small salary with anyone else.

I had in Court circles another amusing friend—though he was usually unintentionally so—Sir Richard Molyneux, a brother of the late Lord Sefton and a Groom-in-Waiting in the 1920s. (He had taken part, with Winston Churchill, in the famous charge at the battle of Omdurman.) Dick seldom thought highly of anyone: most men in his eyes were cads and I cannot, therefore, explain why we ever became friends. He was a generation older, but he used to talk to me a lot in his later years, and he gave me much amusement without realising it.

To give some picture of this unusual character I must jump forward in time for a moment to the Second World War, when

Dick Molyneux was well on in years but undiminished in his peculiarities. In the old Turf Club one evening I was talking to two friends in the outer part of the Smoking Room while he was reading the evening paper standing in front of the fire in the inner sanctum. It was a few weeks after the battle of Alamein. The only other member present was Sir Rupert Beckett, chairman of the Westminster Bank, when to my consternation and delight we heard the unmistakable Molyneux voice, raised to penetrate Rupert Beckett's deafness, proclaim, 'I see that cad Montgomery keeps on advancing!'

Later he came over and said to me, 'By the way, James, do you know this feller Wavell?' I replied, 'Yes, slightly,' and that I had the highest opinion of him as a commander. 'Well,' he said, 'I was down at Windsor the other day with the King and the Queen. They are always very good to me there, don't-cher-know; they always give me the same room looking out towards the Copper Horse. Well, this feller Wavell came to stay and we were all very decent to him, don't-cher-know, but I just wondered ... I meanter-say, is he the sort of feller you'd ask to stay and shoot?' I assured him that he would be on safe ground. 'Talkin' of shootin',' he went on, 'what's happened to everyone? I never see my friends now. Even old Bertie Ancaster never asks me to shoot. Does anyone ask you?' I explained that as there was a major war going on things like shooting (for sport, at any rate) were apt to be a bit disorganised, but he didn't believe much of this and merely thought he was being neglected.

During a severe bombing raid on central London one night, I have been assured, he rang the bell and said to the waiter, 'Tell those fellers upstairs in the billiard-room not to make such a damned noise!'

It was about this time that 'm'old friend' (as he would have said) gave me an awkward moment. The Turf Club had behaved poorly by offering no hospitality to our American allies, but I knew two temporary members of White's who were particularly anxious to see the inside of the Turf and I said I would dine them there. I laid on my friend, Colonel Vesey of the Irish Guards, to make a foursome. We had not been at dinner long when Dick Molyneux entered and coming up to my table said, 'I see you've brought some of your cads from White's round with you.' I could say nothing at the moment, but I followed him and asked him to have a word with me in private. I then explained that he had done a most terrible thing and that they were high-level allies of the V.I.P. class and that he must somehow put things right.

He came back into the room with me and in a matter of two minutes or less had them spellbound and eating out of his hand. He got on to polo and he explained where he used to play good polo in Gloucestershire, but, he added, 'It was no fun really, don't-cher-know, because there was no pop. Well, you can't play polo without pop, can yer?' (He always called champagne 'pop'.) Having charmed the Americans completely he then turned on me and expressed his surprise that two sensible horse-loving men should dine with me, an uncivilised Scot, and a wild Irishman like Tom Vesey; so all was well, at our expense.

Dick had a select collection of girl friends, half his age, whom he took to dinner at the Ritz or Dorchester and to tennis during Wimbledon. My wife was one of these, and, being a non-drinker, she was quite popular. Once, after giving the late Princess Royal dinner at the Ritz, he complained how extraordinary young women had become. 'Not what they were in my day,' he said. 'I took half a bottle of pop with me to the Ritz, don't-cher-know, for myself and I'll be blowed if that young Princess Mary didn't drink half of it—so I had to order another half bottle, and pay for it! Extraordinary!'

We travelled together one very hot Whitsun to visit his nephew, the present Lord Sefton, at Abbeystead in Lancashire. Dick's idea of a journey was to do things in comfort, even if it cost a bit. As I had no car of my own, he explained that I was to pick him up in a hired car in good time for the train, but my luggage must be at his flat in Berkeley Square the day before. His man would proceed in a separate car half an hour ahead of us and would install the luggage and himself and await us.

All worked to plan and our carriage stood empty with all the blinds down, so we were in comfort. Presumably some hundreds of our fellow travellers had shunned the compartment, in the belief that we must be either prisoners on the move, like our present-day train robbers, or lepers. We travelled alone, and not long after we had left London Dick got down a hamper, which he unpacked. It contained sandwiches and minced chicken rolls with two bottles of iced lager beer. 'Sorry,' he said, 'I didn't like to tell my man to pack any pop. It might have looked a bit vulgar, don't-cher-know, if we had had a lot of our fellow citizens sitting all over us.'

We did well enough, but at tea-time I asked him if he would like a drink, as the heat was intense. He asked what I meant to drink and I suggested whisky, if I could get through the crowd to the dining car and get any. 'Filthy stuff,' he said. 'Never touch it. Why not wait for the pop later?' I set off and got some whisky and tepid ginger ale. When we reached Abbeystead we were both given pop, whereupon Dick announced to his nephew, our host and hostess, 'Extraordinary feller, James, don't-cher-know. He has to go clambering along the train in all that heat to get some of his filthy whisky—and now he drinks champagne too.'

To me, he was always a highly entertaining character and, according to my generous host, he stayed on a few weeks after I had left and nearly drank the house out of pop.

To return to my time as a courtier, social life in those days was as rigid as the calendar.

With the rising of Parliament in July the Court left London and followed an inflexible routine. The pattern of functions and engagements had been established long before my day and crystallised into a series of 'hardy annuals'— interrupted only, I imagine, by the First World War: from Cowes to Goodwood, from grouse-shooting in Yorkshire to Balmoral, and so on.

I did one spell of duty at Balmoral. I enjoyed being in a beautiful part of my native country and found Balmoral interesting to see from the inside, but there was not much for a comparatively young member of the staff to do. The King, naturally, had his fixed shoots for his own guests and friends, while we did a little shooting 'for the pot' or took exercise on a golf course which more closely resembled a hayfield. It was a comfortable life and the food was excellent. I also observed and learnt a lot from people like Harry Stonor. Harry was, with the King, one of the crack shots of those days: he taught me a lesson I have never forgotten, and he did it in a characteristic way. We were out for some grouse one day when I heard a whistle from the next butt: it was Harry, warning me of the head-on approach of an old cock grouse. I was about to shoot when the bird fell dead well out in front. Obviously Harry had done it and I afterwards asked him why he had called my attention to it and then shot it himself. 'I wanted to teach you to take your birds further out in front, otherwise you won't have time to make proper use of your second gun.' Of course he was right.

During my Balmoral visit, the annual Ghillies' Ball took place. This was a considerable event and attended by the local lairds as well as the estate people. Only Queen Victoria and John Brown were missing—sad to say. After a bit of dancing and reeling—but not, I hope, literally—I retired to the Equerries' Room in search of refreshment. No one was there, so I got what I wanted and sat down. Within five minutes the door opened and six-foot-three-inches of the immaculate courtier, Stonor, entered quietly, as always. 'James,' he said, 'the Queen expects you to dance the next dance with her', and looking at the programme he added, 'A foxtrot.' 'Really, Harry,' I said, 'Why do you always try to make a fool of me? You know you're pulling my leg.' 'All right,' he said 'I've done my duty and delivered H.M.'s message. The rest is up to you.'

He went away and I thought no more of it, but being bored and alone I decided to go back to the big Hall (plastered with antlers and Landseer's paintings of the Prince Consort and of stags peeping over heather-clad hills) to see what was cooking. To my horror and distress, as the dance was under way, I saw Queen Mary get up from her chair, saying, 'I think this is our dance.' She could not have been kinder to me—as she always was—but regrettably we seemed to be dancing different brands of the then popular foxtrot. She must have suffered, and I did too on her account. However, all things have to end and in due course the music stopped. In the Equerries' Room later all Harry Stonor said to me was: 'Well, I told you so and you ought to have believed me.'

As a Scotsman I was sometimes taken aback, even dazzled, by the 'tartans' I encountered on coming down to breakfast at Balmoral and meeting some of the guests.

Tartans, as we know them today in the shop-windows, are

not old in the way that people are apt to think. Originally, the mills in the North of Scotland turned out tweed of a type which depended on the dyes and wool available to them. Some were really beautiful but they did not in any way resemble the clan tartans as they are known today. Some of Prince Charles Edward Stuart's clothing may still be seen in Edinburgh and elsewhere, but there is no modern 'Stuart' tartan on view, nor to the best of my knowledge did the Prince ever wear the kilt until he had to go into hiding with a price on his head after Culloden.

My brother has at home a painting of the 12th Earl of Moray taking part in the procession to meet the Prince Regent (later George IV) on the first royal visit to Scotland after 1745. The head of my family is carrying part of the regalia: he is dressed in trews and plaids of two or three different brands but none resembles the 'Stuart' cloth of today. The story goes that after the royal visit, not attended by all the Scottish Peers and Chiefs on account of the still strong feeling over the '45 and the 'Butcher' Duke of Cumberland, an enterprising tailor in Princes Street conceived the idea that tartans might be a good new line of business, so he got a mill to turn out patterns and designs and put them in his shop window calling them 'Stuart' tartan since his own name was Stuart! There is now Royal Stuart with a red background, Hunting Stuart, mainly green, and Dress Stuart which is very bright and includes a lot of white. But I will not pursue this story lest some of the great Highland Chiefs turn against me in a bloodthirsty mood.

Within Balmoral, tartans abounded: the carpet would be of one, the curtains of another. In addition, 'Balmoral' tartan was in evidence, although there has never been a clan or family bearing this name. According to the story, Queen Victoria was shopping in Inverness or Aberdeen and happened to notice a certain piece of tweed: she asked what it was and on being told that it was merely an odd piece and that there was no more of it in stock she inquired whether it could be repeated for herself. She was assured that it was worn by no particular family or clan but was just some cloth bought by the shop. And thus, if I am right, 'Balmoral' tartan acquired its name.

It struck me as curious that at Balmoral in my day the Sergeant Footman, as he was called, or top butler, always attended at luncheon or dinner dressed in tail-coat and trousers made of 'shepherd's plaid'. I was told that in the Prince Consort's days he was constantly required to 'stand in' for the Prince while Landseer was painting him. As a result he had no time to change into the conventional starched shirt and black tail-coat and was given permission to appear in the clothes he wore while posing for the artist. I never found any other explanation of how this odd custom came to be and why it should have been continued when the painting was finished; it certainly looked strange in the dining-room at dinner.

I ran into a little trouble when it came to leaving Balmoral. It was the holiday season and I had been asked to stay elsewhere. I had frankly had enough of the idle though pleasant life and I knew I would be much more free, and therefore happier, with my friends. I asked if there would be any objection to my going, imagining they would be quite glad to see the last of me as I was serving no really useful purpose. But I was wrong—and not on account of my *beaux yeux*.

It was a protocol problem. At Balmoral people came and went on fixed days and dates. Every guest was clearly told when to arrive and when he was expected to leave. The King's Equerries and secretaries fulfilled the period allocated to them and were relieved, like sentries, at stated intervals. I alone had no relief, because I was the sole Equerry to a younger son, and was expected to stay indefinitely.

I was advised to seek the advice of the King's Equerry then on duty. He in turn advised me to approach the Master of the Household—who advised me to try the King's Secretary, Sir Clive Wigram. I took all the suggested steps conscientiously but no solution was forthcoming. Clive Wigram sympathised but said that there was nothing he could do. Apparently I was a problem child, proposing something for which there was no precedent. At last Clive Wigram said that the only possible thing would be for me to ask the King in person.

George V was a meticulously punctual man and I knew he would be leaving at ten o'clock next morning to go stalking. At five minutes to ten I was hidden behind a massive statue of the Prince Consort in the hall and when the King appeared I took a nervous step forward and presented myself. Bowing, I expressed the hope that His Majesty would not regard me as unappreciative of his kindness if I were to take my departure shortly because I had been invited to stay elsewhere. He was obviously surprised but very politely said he feared that I had had a rather dull time. I murmured 'Not at all', or something of the sort, and he passed on. But the objective had been achieved. I was permitted to leave shortly afterwards and was very welcome at my destination, thanks to a couple of brace of grouse and a haunch of venison from Balmoral which I had in my car.

My career as a courtier was nearly over now, although I did not know it, but before I left the royal service one event of personal and historical interest took place. In the summer of 1921 the first Royal Air Force Ball was held at the Ritz Hotel and my master, the Duke of York, was the guest of honour, having joined the R.A.F. from the Navy during the war. He gave a small dinner party at the Berkeley and then we walked across to the Ritz. I was on duty, so I saw the party settled in, and then sought out my own friends. Later in the evening H.R.H. came over to me and asked who was the girl with whom I had just been dancing. I told him that her name was Lady Elizabeth Bowes-Lyon and he asked me if I would introduce him, which I did. It was a more significant moment than it was possible then to realise but it is certainly true to say that from then on he never showed the slightest interest in any other young lady and they were married in 1923.

I had no ideas about my future except that I did not intend to—nor could I afford to—remain a courtier all my life. (On my unprincely salary of £450 a year, by the way, I had to maintain a valet!) One day Sir Sidney Greville mentioned to me that if I wished he could get me a job with Lord Cowdray (grandfather of the present one) whose family company, Pearson, had vast and widespread commercial interests. I said I was interested, and the result was that I was offered the opportunity to go into the oil business as a learner at the production end in America, with a view to promotion to higher things after I was trained.

So early in the New Year of 1922 I set off for the unknown, which turned out to be the oilfields of Oklahoma.

VIII

The voyage to New York in the old *Aquitania* was gay and enjoyable. My eldest brother Francis came with me, eager, as I was, to see New York for the first time. But he caught flu and stayed only ten days. Nevertheless in this short time he met and fell in love with a girl called Barbara Murray. Later they were married and when my father died Francis became the Earl of Moray; so his wife became Barbara Moray, thereby reverting—at least phonetically—to her maiden name.

But to return to the *Aquitania*, there were also on board two great friends of mine, American brothers named Alec and Hallam Tuck. Hallam, the elder, was a remarkably able man who had worked in the war for President Hoover's Relief Commission behind the lines while the U.S.A. was still neutral. He later joined the British Army as a gunner. His younger brother Alec came to us in the Royal Scots in France after being wounded at Loos with the King's Own Scottish Borderers. The Tucks were American citizens but they had no hesitation in joining the British Army and obtaining commissions as British citizens because, in their view, America had not entered the war soon enough.

Alec was a character and an adventurer. While I was adjutant of our 2nd Battalion in France I received a letter from him written from Claridge's Hotel in London, announcing his impending arrival on orders from the War Office. He duly arrived, looking very smart and flaunting a large gold cigarette case from Asprey. I was impressed, but later, when I had got to know and like him (and to realise that he had no money at all) I asked how he had managed to stay at Claridge's. 'Oh,' he said, 'I thought it would look more impressive if I wrote to you on their paper, so I just called in to write you that note.'

I then inquired about the magnificent cigarette case. His answer was that he had got it out of pawn for the occasion and on his first leave it would have to return there—if he should survive that long, which he did.

Also aboard the *Aquitania* were the Dolly Sisters, the famous stage twins, with whom we were friends. They had a successful act, in which they appeared in London, Paris and New York, called 'The Dollies and their Collies'. I did not see the collies during the voyage but I saw a lot of Rosie and Jenny Dolly, who were most entertaining, although they never finished a sentence and were always interrupting one another.

The twins were so alike that I never knew which I was speaking to, or how to continue in the morning a conversation of the night before. Neither liked it if I mistook one for the other and as a result I made little progress with them—although they did ask my wife and me to stay with them near Marlow, immediately after our marriage the following year. On balance, I thought it wiser to retreat to Scotland.

My arrival in New York was in one way not very well timed. One of my greatest friends, Napier Sturt (Lord Alington) had been staying with Mrs Cornelius Vanderbilt in her spacious Fifth Avenue mansion. (The house has gone, like the old Ritz Hotel in New York, with the 'developers', but it was comparable in size with, say, Spencer House, St James's.) Napier had grown bored with the grand life and just before my arrival had been reported 'missing' by the Vanderbilt butler. He was traced later to Greenwich Village, where he had 'dug in' with some theatrical friends whose way of life was less formal, not to say Bohemian. The English gentry did not rate very high with Mrs Vanderbilt at that moment.

When I managed to get in touch with Napier the only answer I got was confirmation that he had been bored and that Teddy (Gerrard) and Tallulah (Bankhead) were 'such fun', 'so sweet', and so on. Actually, getting to know some of their set as well as I did, I fancy that more than one fell in love with him and that worse stimulants than drink were resorted to at times.

However, Mrs Vanderbilt had known me in better times, when my address was 'Buck House'—rather than Allerton House, which was the cheapest New York boarding house Alec Tuck could find for us, where we shared one shower and W.C. between our cell-like bedrooms, and where we had to unpack in the cellar and carry up our clothes in laundry baskets to our rooms. But at least I had in Alec a congenial neighbour, ready and willing at any hour of the night to seek adventure and whisky in those ludicrous days of Prohibition, provided only that we could raise a few dollars between us.

Allerton House was not Mrs Vanderbilt's idea of how the well-born British should live but she was kind enough to overlook this (and my association with Napier) and often asked me to lunch or dinner.

On one occasion she gave an enormous dinner and dance in honour of A. J. Balfour, who was on his way home from the Naval Conference at Washington and was staying with the Vanderbilts. I remember the occasion with embarrassment because the only guests who arrived on time were Lord Balfour and myself and together we stood, first on one leg then the other, for forty-five minutes before the company was assembled and dinner could proceed. I was sorry for the charming old man.

The after-dinner dance was, in fact, a costume ball for about 600 people, the ladies wearing white wigs and patches—and very pretty they looked too. After midnight, a nice young American told me he had committed a great blunder. Looking for a place to 'sit out' with his girl friend he had taken her up to the first floor and, opening a door facing the grand staircase, he had been confronted by A. J. B. in his nightshirt, wandering around his vast room which was lit by magnificent chandeliers. The young man apologised profusely, but the guest of honour was quite unperturbed and invited them in, saying, 'You can sit out here all night, so long as you can find how to turn off all these lights for me.'

I fell from grace later by a failure to live up to the expected 'correct' standards of the Vanderbilts. I was asked to a large and very smart luncheon party one Sunday. Not only was I the only male person (in a party of twenty-four) who did not arrive in a top hat and a black tail-coat; but worse, I thought I had a good and original excuse for my late arrival—which was almost true. I entered hurriedly, ushered in by a liveried footman and exclaiming anxiously, 'I'm so sorry, Mrs Vanderbilt, but a tiresome Swedish woman put her head into my room at eleven o'clock this morning and shouted, "If you aren't out of here within half an hour you'll have to make your own bed."' I added (not quite truthfully) that making my bed had made me late, but this—coupled with Napier Alington's recent lapses—finished me, and I was struck off the Vanderbilt visiting list.

My first two months in the United States were spent in the New York office of the Pearson company, the Amerada Petroleum Corporation, deriving its name from the fact that they had interests in both America and Canada. The offices were in the Cunard building, right downtown near the Battery, and a New York banker once said to me that 'she was the best ship Cunard ever built'. I was not clear as to what he meant so he explained that he had helped to finance this—to me—vast edifice.

The Amerada offices were on the 42nd floor and it had been carefully worked out by some of the clerks that it was quickest to board an express elevator to the 40th floor and then either walk on up to the next two storeys or, if lazy, wait for a 'local' elevator to continue the journey up the remaining storeys.

I had to be on the job at 9 a.m. and if I had no time for breakfast (which was quite often) before starting for the office, I would snatch a ham roll and a cup of coffee which was always too hot to drink in the subway station and go on up aloft in a mad rush.

Life here was quite a change from the more comfortable surroundings (and cooked breakfasts) I had been used to at Buck House S.W. One day, when I had been doing my bit of lowly spade-work towards the compilation of the Amerada accounts for the previous year of 1921, I was conducted by the Chief Accountant to my first meeting with an electrical adding machine. He gave me a few words of instruction on how to work the gadget and told me to add up both sides of the balance sheet, with a few extra words in his forceful and unprintable manner to the effect that I had better — — see to it that I got them to balance.

I laboured away, and each time I added a few more hundreds or thousands of dollars the machine made unhappy grinding noises inside its mechanical brain—or soul. At last it disgorged about a yard of paper with all the figures I had fed it and the total at the bottom. But this was only half the battle, for unfortunately a balance sheet has two sides and my concentration had been constantly interrupted by friendly but inquisitive clerks on their way to or from the lavatory, where one could have a few pulls at a cigarette.

I then started off on the equally lengthy addition of the other side of our (to me) unintelligible balance sheet. The machine continued to grind away like a stone-breaker and I had almost lost heart when it eventually belched forth another strip of paper a yard long with the total. It was too much to hope, after all that toil and sweat, that the totals would agree; and the tension inside me was such that I joined those who had gone on ahead to inhale half a Lucky Strike. I would have welcomed a drink but, of course, such a thing was not available. Then, summoning my evaporated courage, I looked at my totals and, believe it or not, they agreed. This seemed too good to be true and I hurried to the private room of the Chief Accountant, where I exulted, saying in effect, 'See what I've done for you! They balance!'

Indeed, alas, it *was* too good to be true. The boss gave my handiwork a cursory glance and pronounced judicially: 'Yes, you've got it to balance, but you are precisely ten million dollars wrong on both sides.' This seemed to be absurd and I did my best to defend the results of my laborious effort. It was no good. 'It's quite simple, Stuart, and don't worry,' the Chief Accountant said. 'You see, the machine is only made to go up to one million and you have omitted the top ten million.'

This only goes to show how easy it is to be fooled or let down by these wonderful mechanical devices and I only hope that the modern computer does better than my old machine in New York.

I was soon sent to Amerada's Oklahoma office in Tulsa, where I got my orders and was then dispatched to the small town of Ardmore, which was the railhead for our operations 'in the field', fourteen miles beyond. I was told in Tulsa to leave my good clothes behind and I arrived at Ardmore in khaki trousers and an open shirt. The reason for this was that if the drillers or 'roustabouts' (the name for casual labourers in the oilfields) were to suspect that I came from the Pearson family office in Whitehall I would be written off as a spy and nobody would teach me anything. I had therefore to pose as one of the unemployed from England 'genuinely seeking work', as the phrase of the time had it. In a sense it was true. I certainly got plenty of work.

We lived in a camp of wooden bunk-houses with no sitting room of any sort. The nearest bath was in Ardmore—fourteen miles away. I decided only to speak when spoken to, but fortunately one of the drillers, a big, friendly man, spoke to me straight away. He told me that he thought I looked 'kind of clean', so he would share a bunk with me. As proof of his insistence on cleanliness he assured me that he always shaved at least once a week. When bedtime came he removed his outer garments and got into our bunk with his underwear still on, which saved him both trouble and the expense of pyjamas. As his underclothes were stained with large discolourations of crude oil I felt that I might not have too much trouble in living up to *his* standards of personal hygiene.

In those days drillers worked twelve-hour shifts, either from midnight to midday or vice versa. This went on for seven days a week, because once a drilling had been started it had to go on, under the old standard rig of those days, all round the clock to avoid the sides of the hole caving in. My bedfellow worked till midnight and went more or less straight to bed. But as I was on the other shift this was my starting time, so that in this Box and Cox manner our sleeping arrangements were made possible.

My routine was to get up about ten o'clock at night, have a large meal, and get to the rig in time to take over at midnight. I got to bed, exhausted, about two o'clock the following afternoon. For one spell of six weeks without a break a driller called Joe, with his tool-dresser and myself, kept up this tough way of life. Joe and I became good friends. He freely offered to teach me anything he could about his highly skilled job and I learned a lot. He also taught me a lot about strong language, which is a large component of every sentence uttered by all oilfield workers I have ever met and is much more diversified than the somewhat repetitive type in constant use in the British Army: but I'm afraid that even in these free-spoken days I cannot give examples here.

Oklahoma oilfield life was hard and so were the men. There was no accommodation for women laid on by the company but a few wives survived in home-made shacks or 'lean-tos' under the occasional scrubby trees. The workers were nomadic and, unlike the British, very mobile. They would jump a freight train any day to go off to a new field in Wyoming, Texas or any state where they had hopes that something good would turn up. They never paid for a railway ticket, regarding it as a waste of good money, and their wives were left to follow on if and when the husband had got a new job—as often as not, I'm afraid, no better than the one before.

The men were of a wide variety of nationalities, with Germans, Italians, Scandinavians and Poles predominating and very few of English extraction. My closest friend was a German policeman's son. His father had left Germany and settled in Wichita Falls, Kansas. The son had joined the U.S. Air Force in the war but had crash-landed so many planes that he had been taken off flying duties. I remember him confiding in me, as a foreigner, with tears in his eyes, how this had practically broken his heart. He had sworn his oath of loyalty to the U.S.A., and meant it, but he was convinced that the U.S. authorities had regarded him as a German enemy in their midst who was deliberately wrecking American machines.

My worst experience in an oilfield was when my driller and friend, Joe, ordered me at dawn one morning to climb up the barely existent steps to the top of the rig, seventy-four feet above us. I did not relish the thought: the act was a hundred times worse. But the pulley at the top, over which the steel cable ran, was cracked and had to be replaced. This disagreeable task fell to me as the learner and no more was said apart from Joe's instructions as to how to execute the job.

I clambered up gingerly and reached the summit. This was a wooden platform, about four feet by three feet, covered in oil and grease and with nothing to hold on to or lean on. There I stood alone, seventy-four feet up and with no support or possibility of help if *in extremis*. Never have I been so frightened. I did not dare to look down or to look anywhere: I knew I must just concentrate or throw myself into space. It was a job for a steeplejack and quite outside any training I had ever had.

The pulley was of steel and so heavy that I could only just manage to lift it up, but about four inches was enough to get it out of its groove. I dropped it down to Joe who was, of course, on the look-out. One direct hit would have killed him and a slip of one foot on my part would have seen me off too. Joe and I were still in touch by means of a cord I had taken up round my waist and he was able to hoist a new pulley up to me. This I had to lift and place in position, then put the steel cable round the pulley.

This—somehow—I managed to do but I was doubtful if I could ever manage the descent. Obviously I did so, but I have only the faintest nightmarish recollection of it. When I reached the ground I was sick. I said to Joe, who had remained calm and motionless throughout, 'Joe, if you ordered me to do that again I couldn't ever in this world. I was never so frightened throughout the war.' He said nothing, but I know he understood.

When I joined the Army in 1914 no one was allowed to shave his upper lip. In Oklahoma the fashion was the reverse, and I alone had a moustache—of the clipped, military variety—regarded as particularly English. It was not long before my fellow-workers decided that it would be a right and proper thing to remove this, and I was held down by three or four toughs while one or two more got to work. Being hopelessly outnumbered (to say nothing of out-muscled) I did not resist, so I emerged from the operation looking even less like Gerald Nabarro than I do normally and the operating 'roustabouts' said I looked much better. Anyway, it gave them a little amusement for half an hour, no bones were broken, and I lived to fight another day.

Another civilised custom to which oilmen objected was the use of a handkerchief except when we went on one of the occasional trips to town—i.e. Ardmore—for a bath. Then a handkerchief was permitted, but on the job in the field it was definitely 'cissy' or 'pansy'—in the idiom of the period. In the open country—and we were surrounded by thousands of acres of scrub and bush—it was unnecessary to dirty a handkerchief when a finger applied to the nose was so effective, and since our sanitary accommodation also extended for unknown acres and square miles, what did it matter?

Throughout most of the year one never wore a coat but our open shirts had two pockets and when in town it was correct to pack a handkerchief on one side and a row of four or five cheap cigars (five or ten cents each) in the other. (Cigarettes were 'pansy' too in those days. In Kansas City I once tried to buy cigarettes and found that the sale of them was, in fact, illegal.

When I had established that I was not a government inspector, however, I was supplied from 'under the counter'.)

The dedicated drillers, like Joe and his friends, never smoked at all because of the danger of fire if they should strike gas, which usually preceded any oil-producing well. But they chewed tobacco day and night and in the process chewed their back teeth down to the roots. They had the teeth replaced with gold ones, which were not only practical for chewing purposes but were also regarded as a sound investment as they were difficult, not to say impossible, to steal.

Chewing tobacco necessitates a lot of spitting but the men became so practised in this art that they would almost always hit the top of the twelve-inch or ten-inch pipe in the middle of the floor of the derrick, or rig, at a distance of ten or twelve feet. They were really very neat and tidy about it.

We had few relaxations, but the work was so tiring that sleep took up most of our spare time. After pay-days there was some poker played while the money lasted. The chief spending was on corn whisky straight from the still. It is horrible stuff drunk at full strength and to dilute it only prolongs the agony. I abstained for two months and drank nothing at all, but then I went back to it because the life was so monotonous and boring.

Every three weeks three or four of us would go into Ardmore to have a bath and supper. One day a pleasant young man asked me if I would like to go in with him and go to an evening party at the house of his aunt. With the kind of social life I was having, I jumped at the invitation. On the way he asked me what I had been doing before leaving England. I found this hard to answer; to explain about my time in royal circles was impossible, so I said I had been a 'sort of secretary' to somebody. He chewed this over for a little and then said, 'See here, Jim, I don't think I would say anything to my aunt about that job if I were you. She's kind of particular.'

I agreed willingly and the evening passed off very well. The story also gave my father much pleasure when my next letter reached him.

Oklahoma has always been a dry state (in the alcoholic sense) on account of the so-called American Indians who live in reservations there. It is an offence to sell them hard liquor, which is reputed to affect them disastrously. Apart from the corn whisky I have mentioned it was practically impossible to get anything to drink—certainly anything worth drinking—in the whole state. There was, however, one exception, when an Episcopalian parson asked me if I would go to evening service in his church in Ardmore and then have supper at the vicarage.

I did so, and, for my benefit, they sang a hymn to the tune of 'God Save the King'. But what was even more surprising was that at supper he produced a bottle of quite palatable Burgundy and when I asked how he came by it he answered: 'Well, you see, I can apply for so many bottles according to the number of communicants in my parish. I always put in for the best and I have opened one for your visit.' I couldn't help asking him how he dealt with his parishioners, to which he replied unhesitatingly, 'Oh, I give them that bottled grapejuice which is like the real thing in colour and they don't know the difference because they've never tasted wine.' I was rather shocked at the time.

The absence of friends and the inability to see even anyone from one's own country was what I disliked most. In the Army one had been with friends, whether serving abroad or not, and in New York I had a few, but the only Englishman I ever saw in Oklahoma was the Chief Accountant from the New York office, who made one visit while I was there and took me into Ardmore for supper.

A rich old American in New York once asked me about my life in the Middle West. He then said that he had visited most states but never thought of going to such a place. He added, 'When I was young—before Oklahoma entered the Union—the State of Kansas was celebrated for its sunshine, sunflowers and S.O.B.s: but now that Oklahoma has become a state, Kansas is only celebrated for sunshine and sunflowers!'

In April 1923 I obtained permission from Pearson's to go home on leave. My return from New York was on board the *Berengaria*, another Cunarder but originally German-built and taken over by us after 1918 as a part of German reparations. The Dolly Sisters happened to be on board again, so that friendship was renewed, and another fellow-passenger was Gladys Cooper, whom I came to know much better at a later date as a result of my friendship with her first husband, Captain Herbert Buckmaster—'Buck'—who founded Buck's Club in Clifford Street at the end of the First

World War and remained its life and soul until his death in 1966. But I mention Miss Cooper now for a particular reason.

Among my acquaintances on board was a well-to-do American who was carrying a soft leather bag containing 100 British gold sovereigns, his fear being that in an uncivilised country like England he would need enough gold with him to convince the Ritz Hotel that he could pay for his board and lodging. I don't know how many sovereigns were left to him when we docked at Southampton but I do know that I was in possession of twelve due to his continuing losses at bridge. No man could have been more good-natured and he took his losses as a matter of course. He always had two bottles of champagne on ice in the smoking room bar, two in the restaurant, and two more in the bathroom off his cabin, so we were never thirsty for long.

My new friend expressed a desire to have the honour of giving a dinner party for Gladys Cooper. This was organised and six of us dined together. At one point Miss Cooper was complaining about the theatrical producers in New York but her host, fatigued perhaps by his hours at the bridge table and the bar, was taking a rest. Gladys was expressing with animation her desire to play 'The Second Mrs Tanqueray' in America when our host rallied and, feeling it to be time for him to contribute to the conversation, joined in with, 'But do tell me, Miss Cooper, who was the *first* Mrs Tanqueray?'

When this cheerful voyage ended I had no idea that my American career was over too. The intention had been that after my leave I should return to Oklahoma and the oilfields, and in due course, perhaps, earn promotion to a less rugged sphere of the industry. But unpredictable events decreed otherwise, as I shall explain, and my life changed course drastically once again.

IX

Soon after I came home from America on leave in June 1923, Stanley Baldwin, who succeeded Bonar Law as Prime Minister and Leader of the Conservative Party, made a famous speech at Plymouth which rocked the political boat from bow to stern. I supposed Baldwin realised the effect his speech would have in the country, but for the man in the Top Job he took a grave risk, although I am sure he believed in the policy he suddenly advocated. The risk was the greater because he was a new and little-known leader. Anyhow, what he said caused grave discomfort and anxiety in the Party.

Baldwin wanted to get authority to protect our industries and employment in them by the application of certain tariffs or import duties. It was apparently his view—and I did not dissent— that it is better to enjoy a steady weekly wage, even if the cost of living rises slightly, than to have no wage at all and to be forced to resort to 'the dole' as it was then called, or public assistance. But obviously the old cry 'Your food will cost you more' was raised all over the country. Baldwin had to ask for a dissolution of Parliament to test opinion in the country. The election took place late in 1923.

I had never for a moment entertained any thought of standing for Parliament. In the summer of 1923 my marriage to Rachel Cavendish took place and soon afterwards I was at Doune Lodge in Perthshire with my father when to my complete surprise I received a telegram from the headquarters in Elgin of the Unionist Association of Moray and Nairn, asking me if I would allow my name to go forward as their candidate for the constituency of Moray and Nairn. Nothing could have been farther from my thoughts and I told my father merely as a matter of interest. To my utter surprise, not to say consternation, he said why didn't I 'have a shot'. It wouldn't do me 'any harm', and it would be 'an experience'.

It was, of course, understood that I hadn't a hope of being elected as the Liberals were well entrenched and had held the seat for about a quarter of a century.

In this spirit I accepted and soon afterwards set out for my first adoption meeting in Elgin, spending a bad night in Aberdeen on the way rehearsing my first-ever political speech for the meeting next day.

I don't remember much about the meeting except that I was adopted; during the following weeks of constant meetings and general electioneering I often regretted it.

About a week before Polling Day my election agent in Elgin said to me as we were going wearily to bed after a long day, 'They're saying in the pubs that you may be elected next week.' I was very tired and I'm afraid I turned on the poor man and told him in no uncertain terms not to talk such rubbish, adding, 'I have a job in America and I have to get back to it.'

Yet win I did. To say it was unexpected, so far as I and a good many other people were concerned, is an understatement. But I was elected with a majority of 1,027 votes and obviously it was out of the question to resign in the next breath, so all thoughts of going back to the U.S.A. had to be abandoned.

But my Party as a whole was less lucky than I was. The Conservatives lost their majority; no party obtained a majority and the Liberals, under their ageing leader, Mr Asquith, held the balance of power. Baldwin resigned at once and Ramsay MacDonald (whose home was in Lossiemouth, by the way, and who therefore was and remained for the rest of his life a constituent of mine) formed the first Labour Government of Great Britain with the support of the Asquithian Liberals—while it lasted.

In this short Parliament I had the interesting experience of hearing Mr Asquith, as Liberal leader, making his far-reaching speech in which he gave his party's support to the first Labour Government. I do not question his sincerity but the effect on his own party has been argued for a generation. My own belief is that Lloyd George's 'coupon election' of 1918 and Asquith's support of the Socialists in 1923 combined to lose for the Liberal Party the popularity which they had enjoyed for so long.

In fact the Liberal-supported Labour Government lasted eleven months, when we had to fight another General Election. At this

1924 election I did genuinely want to hold my seat if only to prove that my unexpected win the previous year was not a mere flash in the pan. I held it quite easily, in the absence of a Liberal, and continued to do so with satisfactory majorities until I retired in 1959—thirty-five and a half years without a break, which only goes to show, if it shows anything, how surprising life can be and how inscrutable is Fate!

This election returned the Tory Party to power and kept it in office under Stanley Baldwin till 1929.

Mr Asquith, or Lord Oxford and Asquith as he later became, was, I think, the most perfect and polished speaker I have ever had the pleasure of hearing. He was always word-perfect and apparently imperturbable, yet (although I did not know him personally) I have been told that in discussing how to control those ghastly 'speaker's nerves' that afflict nearly everybody, he remarked that no one would make a good speech unless his system was riddled with nerves.

My first meeting with a political leader was several years before I entered Parliament or had any thought of doing so. He was Lord Balfour (whom I have already mentioned in my New York experiences) and the occasion was when, not long after I left the Army, I was staying at Polesden Lacy, near Dorking, with Mrs Ronald Greville, almost the last of the great Edwardian hostesses. Balfour had resigned as Prime Minister and Leader of the Conservative Party some thirteen years earlier—in 1905, when I was a schoolboy.

He was a man of infinite charm and unquestioned intelligence but I believe he was never a great leader. I heard Sir Edward Carson say, when he too was in retirement, that Balfour's failing, if it may be called that, was that he always saw so clearly the other side (or sides) to any question. The result of his perfect logic and reasoning was, therefore, inclined to be indecision, which is fatal for a party leader. Ordinary men can back a horse each way, but a leader cannot: he has to make a decision and lead his party, for better or worse, over a chosen course, whatever the hazards. Balfour was, however, also a very fine debater—and I have heard that view expressed by a man with some knowledge of the subject, Winston Churchill. From what he told me, I fancy that Winston feared him. Balfour would rise to his feet in the Commons with

71

his few notes written on the backs of five or six long envelopes and proceed to tear the opposing forces to ribbons.

At Polesden Lacy I had to partner Lord Balfour at tennis. Although it is now forty-five years ago I remember vividly that I had to run about and do a great deal of work up at the net while Lord Balfour defended, with remarkable ability, our backline, driving and lobbing with the consistent skill of long practice. As a team we fared quite well and as we came off the court he said to me, 'Stuart, do you play bridge?' I replied guardedly that I had played a good deal, probably badly, in my regiment (where at least it was cheap) and that I knew the rules. 'Very well,' he said, 'you will be my partner after dinner. Don't forget!' I was flattered, but I admit that I had no idea until later that there was any ulterior motive.

After dinner Mrs Greville who, as usual during the week-ends of the so-called 'season', had a large and distinguished party, said to Lord Balfour, 'I do hope you will come and talk to the ladies, they are so anxious to meet you.' His reply was, 'I'm very sorry but I'm playing bridge with my friend Stuart.' Hostesses like Mrs Greville had seen too much of male idiosyncrasy to try persuasion and merely acquiesced when Lord Balfour suggested that any two men of the party should come into the next room and complete our four.

There was no cutting for partners; I had simply been designated. Lord Balfour did not trouble to score (I doubt if he knew how to) and it was politely indicated that I should take on the job. I think we played two rubbers. More than once in a single hand I had to remind my partner what suit we were playing, even when he had called and was playing the hand. Finally, having checked the score with our opponents, he simply said to me, 'How much did we lose, Stuart?' I replied, 'I regret, sir, that we lost ten shillings each.' 'Very cheap at the price' were his last words as he left the room to go upstairs to bed. And neither we nor the ladies saw him again until lunch next day.

He continued to pursue similar evasive tactics. At one point I asked him, in my politest manner, why, with all his knowledge and experience, he had not weighed in the previous night after dinner even if only to contradict or correct some of the younger men who were talking at random. He said he preferred to listen to, and learn from, the young, but that he had no wish to argue.

72

Another characteristic attitude of Lord Balfour's was that he saw no need to read the newspapers, because 'any man of intelligence' could pick up all the essential information in the course of conversation by lunch-time. A very different character from Winston Churchill who, as Prime Minister, had the morning papers delivered after midnight and got through about half a dozen before he would go to bed.

After the 1918 Armistice Balfour went to Paris as second string to the Prime Minister, Lloyd George, to negotiate the Peace Treaty with Germany. They were so ill-assorted a couple that I could not refrain from asking A.J.B. one day how he had got on with Ll.G. He gave me one of his typically courteous but evasive replies. He admitted that the P.M. upset his plans at times by sending for him just when he intended to play tennis, but that it was more or less simple otherwise because he 'could understand the P.M.'s "French"'.

It was Carson who told me of the day when he was called to No. 10 by Lloyd George and asked to take the Admiralty. At the time this did not suit Carson, who suggested Reginald McKenna instead. Bonar Law was summoned but no decision was reached. The P.M. was very busy so he said to Bonar Law, 'You go over to Carlton Gardens and ask Balfour's advice.' Looking at the clock, he added, 'He'll be in his bath, I expect, by now but you can talk through the door.'

Carson said he knew in advance what the answer would be and, sure enough, in half an hour Bonar Law was back. Ll.G. asked what Balfour had said and Law replied, 'Well, he *was* in his bath but he said he thought that either would do very well at the Admiralty.' So Carson did not have to accept.

A friend of mine, an old Lobby correspondent of the *Scotsman*, once told me that Balfour was the nearest thing to a complete fatalist he had ever met. He recalled that when he wanted to talk to him about the Irish situation but had missed him in the House he hurried after him to No. 4 Carlton Gardens. Balfour was then under police protection for fear of Sinn Fein violence, but, seeing a light on, the journalist rang the bell and knocked. He heard the soft pad of carpet slippers approaching and the door was opened in person by A.J.B., who poked his head out and said, 'Well, have you come to shoot me?'

Balfour was a purist about the English language but his devotion to purism ruined the effectiveness of a meeting of his in Aberdeen. It was a true-blue Conservative Party mass meeting where all were prepared to cheer any statement of Tory policy, however stale and obvious. Balfour got himself involved in the middle of a sentence about Ireland. He stopped in mid-stream and leaning down towards the Press below the platform said, 'Cut that out please. I'll start that bit again.'

As a statesman he may well have been right to ensure getting the record correct, but nothing can be more damaging to the reception of any speech than to have a paragraph interrupted by the great orator himself. But then people can make tactical errors while speaking that haunt them for ever. Baldwin said of himself that the silliest thing he ever did was when he evaded an issue by saying that his lips were sealed.

The first political leader I knew well was, of course, Stanley Baldwin. It was through the late Lord Halifax (then Edward Wood) that I was first introduced to Baldwin. He asked me to dine with him in Eaton Square and to my surprise seated me next to Baldwin. Being young and shy, I had little or nothing to say and I did not want to bother an important and busy man with trivialities. However, he did not forget me and we talked together fairly often in the Smoking Room of the House.

It is not every political leader who finds time to spare for young back-benchers (I was twenty-six when I entered the House) but he was always charming to me. He was indeed an unusual and remarkable man in many ways. He gave the impression of great calm, but he also gave the impression of indolence. He did not laugh much, but he never got angry. There is no doubt that he had 'something' but it is something I cannot define. He could be tough, as when he defended himself against tough critics and opponents—for example, the Beaverbrook and Rothermere newspapers. His description of the Press Barons as seeking 'power without responsibility—the prerogative of the harlot through the ages' has never been forgotten.

I remember one conversation I had alone with him in the Smoking Room not long before the Abdication of Edward VIII—though that sensational event had not yet even cast a shadow so far as the public was concerned. He told me how sorry he was for the King. Then, apparently digressing, he remarked that he was very lonely in his job as P.M., adding, 'You see, there are only three or four people whom I can take into my complete confidence and trust them never to say anything outside.' But, he went on, he might be kicked out at any time, or could, if he so desired, resign office, whereas the King was there for life. 'And', he added, 'he's alone—a very lonely life. He should have a wife in whom he can confide.'

My friend and mentor, David Margesson (the late Lord Margesson whom I eventually succeeded as Chief Whip in 1941) once told me that Baldwin's strength lay in the fact that he only 'ticked over' normally at half speed and was therefore capable of 'revving up' his engines at any time and bringing into play great reserves of energy. I also remember Winston Churchill once saying to me, 'Baldwin was the best Party manager the Tories ever had.'

There were many unexpected aspects to Baldwin's character, mostly arising out of his quiet, often unspoken determination to pursue his own course undeterred by criticism or by any thought of 'what people would say': most criticism, I suspect, he regarded as frivolous, ignorant or partisan—or all three; no doubt there was a good deal of 'I know best' about him, but he didn't shout it from the house-tops. He was the last Prime Minister to pack his bags and disappear to Aix-les-Bains for the whole of August every year. He insisted, too, on his Ministers getting proper breaks from duty at their desks and from constant attendance at Cabinet meetings.

One personal experience I had of his unorthodoxy was when I accompanied him on a trip to Scotland (after I had become Scottish Unionist Whip). He had to address a large Party gathering in Lanarkshire. He had all the trappings—secretaries and dispatch boxes, etc.—but after breakfast he sent the staff off to Glasgow to accompany Mrs Baldwin, who had to launch a ship on the Clyde. I was kept in attendance in case he wanted anything.

I was writing in the hall of the house where we were staying and imagined the great man to be immersed in his official boxes, but at about 11 a.m. he came to me and asked if I was very busy. I said I was merely replying to some of the endless letters which any M.P. gets, but not really 'busy'. He then asked me to come into his room and said, 'James, do you think our host would think it very awful of me if I had a whisky and soda at this hour of the day?' I replied that I was sure it would be all right and that I would get it. 'But on one condition only,' he said. 'That you have one with me.' I admitted that I could manage that too.

He then began to talk, eyeing his red boxes with obvious distaste, and asked me whether I thought that his audience that afternoon would prefer him to speak from the Foreign Office and other briefs contained in the boxes—which he did not appear to have opened—or to tell them something of his own thoughts and feelings regarding the general situation. It should be remembered that Hitler had now been in power for two or three years and that things were beginning to warm up internationally. (In fairness, be it also remembered that Mr Baldwin had, not long before, issued the Government's first official White Paper on rearmament.) I told the P.M. that I was sure the audience would prefer an expression of his own personal views delivered 'off the cuff'. I think this caused him some relief and indeed, if I am right, this may be regarded as an indication of that indolence to which I have referred.

Having finished our 'small refreshment' (as we call a drink in Scotland) I said I would leave him as I knew how busy he must be with his papers, and with a speech to make soon after lunch. As I was leaving the room, he called to me, 'Here, before you go, give me one of those newspapers. It doesn't matter whether it's the *Scotsman* or the *Glasgow Herald*.' I gave him one and returned to my letters, assuming he was studying the foreign news. But twenty-five minutes later he opened the door and threw the paper at me saying, 'There, that's not bad. I did the crossword in twenty-five minutes.' Still no work on the speech and only forty-five minutes to go before a luncheon party.

He barely spoke a word to anyone at lunch; he was deep in thought and obviously a bundle of nerves. But he made the speech well enough, speaking for about fifty minutes from one little bit of paper twisted round his first finger: he had a curious habit of appearing to kiss his notes while speaking. It was not a great speech but, having got it off his chest, he was a different man—

relaxed and ready to talk to anyone in the room whether friend or total stranger.

(Winston Churchill's methods were totally opposite: his worries were during the composition of any big speech. After dictation and revision, he would enjoy a hearty meal, probably washed down with a little tonic in the form of champagne, and then go on to the platform—with full notes, of course, but word-perfect.)

Before leaving Stanley Baldwin, I cannot help jumping forward to 1942 to recall that it was I who brought him and Winston Churchill together after six years or so of strained relations. The three of us lunched alone at No. 10. They discussed an attack which the P.M. proposed to launch in the House against Ireland for refusing us the use of her bases. Baldwin told him he would only irritate the Irish, and the P.M. took his advice. Afterwards Baldwin refused the P.M.'s offer of a cigar and lit his usual pipe, explaining that he had long ago given up cigars because he could not afford them. To this his host, stuffing about twelve inches of cigar into his face, rejoined: 'Oh, I flatter myself that I have democratised cigars!'

I have already admitted to a lack of political ambition, and during my early years in the House—until 1935 when I became a Whip—I cannot claim to have played a very active part in parliamentary affairs. Also there was the fact that I had two sons (born in 1924 and 1925) to educate, followed by a daughter born seven years later. It was far from easy for a man who had to earn a living and bring up a young family to attend the House assiduously and look after his constituency affairs as well. As for most of those years we had good working majorities there was less strain than there is for a young M.P. today, but on the other hand he is much better rewarded, for in those days we had an 'allowance' (later called 'salary') of £400 a year, the amount which had been approved in Lloyd George's day, and very little by way of reimbursement of our unavoidable expenses.

I went to work for a well-known firm of City stockbrokers, Messrs J. and A. Scrimgeour, where I remained for twelve years. Thus I travelled to the City each morning and then to Westminster in the afternoon. The rest of the day—and night—depended on the parliamentary business in hand, but often one was in attendance until 11 p.m., when the House normally rose, or much later if required. Some evenings one was able to go home or to one's club to dinner and return at eleven o'clock to vote. (It is ten o'clock nowadays.)

Although I frequented the Smoking Room and enjoyed the free-for-all conversation (privileged by an unwritten rule) which gave one a pretty good idea of the way the wind was blowing among the rank and file of all parties, I did not have (nor did I seek) many friends in high places. Apart from the Prime Minister (Baldwin, who, as I have mentioned, was a regular visitor to the Smoking Room) and David Margesson, my friends really consisted of a handful of my fellow Scotsmen, notably Jack Gilmour (Sir John Gilmour, then Scottish Whip and later Secretary of State for Scotland) and Sir Robert Horne (later Viscount Horne, and one-time Chancellor of the Exchequer), from all of whom I learned a lot.

In 1935 I was sent for by David Margesson and told that he and the P.M. wanted me to take over the post of Scottish Whip owing to the sudden death of Sir Frederick Thomson, M.P. for South Aberdeen. He gave me about half an hour to think it over. I was taken completely by surprise as I had never contemplated any such thing in my life.

The P.M. saw me alone at seven o'clock that evening in his room in the Commons and asked me to accept. I told him that I was ignorant, but that I did wish to help if I could. However, I had to explain that I was about to leave in the morning for Athens to join an American friend sailing to Constantinople and that I could not cancel the trip at so late an hour as I couldn't even get in touch with my friend who was then in mid-ocean between Malta and Athens. I had told Margesson of this in advance and he had, of course, warned the P.M. In fact he had told the P.M. that he wanted me in the Whips' Room at once and that I must on no account be allowed to go on holiday. But again Baldwin did the unexpected. He said, 'James, will you take my advice?' I said I would if it were possible. 'Well then,' he said, 'go to Athens tomorrow. You may never get another chance. Join the Whips' Office on your return.'

The Whips were annoyed, but I got my holiday and, on my return, I became a Whip, and remained one for the next twelve years.

X

The word 'Whip' suggests violence or cruelty or chastisement, but only the third of these could be said to have any connection with the activities of a Parliamentary Whip and even then the punishment is never physical. The name was originally 'Whipper-in', and the basic function of a Party Whip is to ensure that every possible member of his party is in attendance at the House when required.

'Whip' is also applied to the written message the Whips send out to their Members. The urgency of the need for attendance is indicated by the number of underlinings and the well-known phrase 'a three-line Whip' indicates that the summons is of maximum importance and a member who fails to respond to it without a good and sufficient reason does so at his peril, so far as his relationship with his Parliamentary Party is concerned. The Government Chief Whip in the House of Commons has the official title of Parliamentary Secretary to the Treasury and his colleague the Chief Whip in the House of Lords is the Captain of the Gentlemen-at-Arms. The Deputy Chief Whip in the Commons is the first of the junior Lords of the Treasury.

The public, as readers of the popular Press, cannot be blamed if they regard Whips—and Chief Whips in particular—as inhuman, heartless bullies, devoid of friends, living a life apart and exercising dictatorial powers over a large number of amiable, intelligent and devoted Members of Parliament. There are those critics who seem to be convinced that if only the Whips could be got rid of (hanged or burnt alive, perhaps) all would be well in Britain and perhaps further afield. In my experience, Whips are dedicated men who devote their whole time to the House while it is sitting and much of their remaining time to their constituencies. They rarely see their homes in the evening.

It should be realised, too, that Whips possess no occult power and rely on their ability to handle men and to get on with them. Whips are picked because they have friends rather than enemies in their own party, and because of their local territorial interests— e.g. London or Scotland or the North and West of England; and/or because of their particular interests and knowledge—e.g. foreign affairs, finance, agriculture, labour questions, and so on. As a last resort, if (to quote Sir Kenneth Pickthorn questioning a later Chief Whip, Martin Redmayne, before a Select Committee) the awkward M.P. insists on being 'a cad'—or defying the Party's line—the Chief Whip may threaten to take away the Whip from him. In practice this means that the M.P. is expelled from the Party, though not, of course, from Parliament. Such excommunication may well worry the Member because the local Party Association in his constituency then has a free hand to adopt a new candidate, ready to support the Party at the next election. However, this drastic remedy is not lightly applied, because the Party vote will be split and an opposing candidate may win the seat on a minority vote. Therefore the withdrawal of the Whip is not, obviously, a method of discipline to which Chief Whips and the Leader of the Party will resort without much care and thought. Indeed I think it is true that David Margesson never, in all his years as Chief Whip, took the Whip away from anyone, despite the fact that he enjoyed the reputation of a tyrannical and ruthless Whip—which, by the way, is nonsense.

During my own time as Chief Whip, to jump ahead for a moment, I did once take the Whip away from a Member. It affected the seat of Marylebone. I had been subjected to grave provocation, and seeing the Member in question go the wrong way at Division time I immediately rang up Mr Churchill, as Leader of the Party, and asked if he would agree to my withdrawing the Whip. Churchill didn't go in for half measures: after no more than a minute's talk and thought, he said, 'Yes, take it away and tell the Press at once, before he gets at them.' Incidentally, with Sir Wavell Wakefield as candidate, we held the seat at the next election.

Whips can, of course, be rude to Members, but this is harmless enough and spills no blood. Members, in return, can be rude to Whips, which is fair enough.

Ladies in the House of Commons are a particular problem here: some of them cheat magnificently, as Lady Astor did, and it is very

80

difficult, in spite of their claims to equality, to address them in the same terms one applies regularly to male Members. I found they didn't like it at all even though I always cut out the worst of my vocabulary when dealing with them.

I did tell Nancy Astor once many years ago that it was no worse to accept a contribution from the brewers, whom she opposed as evil men who traded in the demon drink, than to live on the rents paid to her husband by the brothel keepers of New York. This, however, she took very well and merely said that she would appeal to Mr Speaker for protection. I must say she never bore me malice and I got much pleasure from our arguments about religion, alcohol and prostitution in particular. In principle, she was admirable but in practice she was usually wrong. She was very kind to me but I did think at moments that if I had possessed the Astors' wealth I could have been more open-handed. I once, for instance, accompanied her to a Trade Fair and she gave me a waste paper basket! (I in fact still use the basket, which is quite a good one; and after all, she had to buy something.)

Lest anyone think my remarks about Nancy Astor ungenerous, I would like to record one anecdote to square the account. The Duke of Windsor—then the Prince of Wales—was, and is, a keen golfer and he entered regularly, as I did, for the Parliamentary Golf Handicap. The event took place at Walton Heath and H.R.H. had already got into the last four, while Nancy Astor and I were playing each other for the same position. The news reached us on the course that the Prince had won his match, so that the winner of ours would have to play him in the semi-final. I said to Nancy, 'Listen to me—you enjoy publicity and you are rich. You will get lots of publicity in a match against H.R.H. I am ready to sell you the game for £5.'

She very properly refused and told me to get on with the game. Shortly afterwards I reached the proud if dangerous position of two up with three holes to go. I shanked into a bunker at the 17th instead of taking an easy approach to the green. Then we were all square on the 18th, and I lost the 19th; but instead of the fiver I received next day an expensive golfing coat which Nancy had bought for me at Fortnum and Mason. Thus we both got what we wanted, which is an unusual thing in life.

I know that I lay myself open to the charge of some bias in

favour of Whips but I stand by my considered view that their aim and object in life is to maintain stability of government, and that without some such body of dedicated men, who sacrifice most of their home life and other interests to the job, there would be chaos.

The Party organisation and the Whips' Office have gradually grown up since the eighteenth century, and it is worth remembering that Disraeli, for one, held the view that the necessary preservation of stability in running the nation's affairs could not be maintained without a Whips' Office; while Mr Churchill himself—no great Party man—remarked to me once in the mid-1940s, 'I do not know how I could have managed without that solid rock of support on which I have been able to rely in these dangerous years.'

In my role of Scottish Whip in the (National) Government of 1935–7, under the premiership of Stanley Baldwin, I did my job to the best of my ability; but while I was of course closely involved, parliamentarily, with the affairs of the day I had no sufficiently intimate, personal connection with the big events to justify my retracing now the steps of so many other writers, political and historical.

At home, the highlight of the period was the Abdication of Edward VIII at the end of 1936. Within two weeks of the coronation of his brother, George VI, in May 1937, Baldwin resigned in favour of Neville Chamberlain. The new Prime Minister became also, of course, Leader of the Conservative Party, and as such (to drop to a much lower level of political significance) invited me to become Deputy Chief Whip to David Margesson, as well as continuing as Scottish Whip. This promotion brought me the advantages of learning a great deal more and of bringing me into more regular contact with senior Ministers.

No man in politics ever had a better friend or a more competent lieutenant than had Stanley Baldwin in Neville Chamberlain. He was highly efficient and one could not wish for a better chairman of a meeting or committee. He was also admired and respected by the Party; but unfortunately he could not mix easily with people, and he aroused more dislike on the Opposition benches than is normal between a Tory P.M. and the Labour Members.

In a way this was the result of a quality which distinguished him—that chilling scorn he used when dealing with Opposition attackers; in fact, when on his best form in exposing Socialist fallacies, he got under the skin of some of the Members opposite to a quite remarkable degree. But this was simply his natural manner; he lacked Baldwin's sympathetic touch.

Chamberlain did not follow Baldwin's practice of frequenting the Smoking Room and making contact with back-benchers. One evening Alec Douglas-Home (then Lord Dunglass) asked some of us to look into the Smoking Room before dinner because he was bringing the P.M. in and wanted a few friendly souls to rally round. Alec was Neville's Parliamentary Private Secretary at the time and felt that the P.M. ought, like his predecessor, to meet, informally, more of the men whose Leader he was.

About eight or ten of us gathered together and conversation admittedly dragged a bit, though we managed to get going to some extent on fly-fishing, which was Neville's great love. In spite of our efforts, however, it was not a great success and, as I was leaving the room, my Socialist friend, James Maxton, came up to me and said, 'Ach, Jimmy, ye'll have to do better than that. Anybody could see how unhappy ye all were.'

We certainly did not succeed in getting the new P.M. to frequent the friendly Smoking Room. I think he realised his shortcomings, which were undoubtedly due to shyness and in no way detracted from his many admirable qualities.

I am writing personal reminiscences and not a serious political history from documents or even diaries, so I will not re-hash the events and difficulties besetting Neville Chamberlain in his approaches to Hitler during the months immediately preceding the declaration of war in 1939 (or the setbacks and disasters later, which I believe would have had to be faced by any Prime Minister at the time).

Chamberlain was only doing what he believed to be right in our interests and to avoid war. His approach may have been wrong and, admittedly, he failed: probably he thought that the word of other Heads of State must mean as much to them as his word did to himself, and it is only fair to him to recall that when he returned from Munich and stated publicly that peace would be preserved he was loudly applauded in Parliament and by vast numbers of the public.

I was glad to see, some time ago, that a son of Neville Chamberlain's came to his father's defence in the Press on a point about which I have my own views. Anthony Eden (Lord Avon) records in his memoirs an occasion at dinner at No. 10 Downing Street when the P.M.'s son and also his brother, Sir Austen Chamberlain, were present. The conversation was on foreign affairs (Eden was Foreign Secretary) and Eden writes that Sir Austen remarked, 'But, of course, Neville, you're not supposed to know anything about foreign affairs.' Sir Austen was, of course, a former Foreign Secretary and obviously he was being flippant. I am sure the implicit reference was to the well-known fact that Joseph Chamberlain, when his sons were young, had coached Austen, the elder, for a political career and Neville for the family business, though like other 'best laid plans' this one 'went agley' and it was the younger brother who unpacked his bags at No. 10. I believe also that the remark was made because at the table was a Foreign Secretary who prided himself on being the world's greatest living expert on foreign affairs! But how Anthony Eden, knowing the Chamberlain background, could have taken this light-hearted aside of Sir Austen's seriously is beyond my comprehension.

Mentioning Austen Chamberlain tempts me to linger for a moment on that curiously interesting man. He held many high offices, including the Treasury and the Admiralty as well as the Foreign Office, where he was responsible for our negotiations culminating in the Locarno Treaty with France and Germany in 1925. He signed the Treaty with Briand representing France and Stresemann Germany. On his way back to London he stayed with Lord Crewe, our Ambassador in Paris. He was, of course, asked to meet the French Press at the Embassy to talk about what had been achieved at Locarno. Doubtless the French journalists assigned to this conference could speak English, but Sir Austen prided himself on his knowledge of the French tongue. Knowledge of a language, however, does not necessarily include its colloquial peculiarities. He started off by describing the scene at Locarno and his meeting with Stresemann and Briand. However, he added that when he greeted Stresemann *'nous nous sommes baisés'*, an unfortunate phrase which in colloquial French has distinct homosexual implications.

A small incident concerning Sir Austen has always stayed in my mind. I once asked his advice as to how to answer a difficult correspondent; I added apologetically that there did usually seem to be two sides to any question, to which he answered, 'The trouble is that there are usually *more* than two. If there were no more than two sides it would be simpler.'

Austen Chamberlain was a respected and trusted leading figure in the Conservative Party—and a great House of Commons man—for many years, but there was truth in what Winston Churchill said of him afterwards—and not unkindly: 'Poor Austen. He always played the game and always lost it.'

Maybe Harold Wilson's father had clearer foresight than Joe Chamberlain when he photographed his son as a little boy standing outside No. 10 Downing Street. The way to No. 10 has many pit-falls; as Winston Churchill once remarked to me on this subject when we were discussing the merits and weaknesses of the up-and-coming Conservative members, 'What they don't realise is that it's not a flat race, but a steeplechase course.'

I am not pretending to be wise after the event, but I was not happy about Neville Chamberlain's 'good news' which he announced on his return from his final visit to Hitler. But Neville was an honest man and I do not find it so strange that our Prime Minister took the word of another Head of State that he would adhere to a certain course of action. I was with him, in my capacity as Deputy Chief Whip, when he made his brief statement from an upper window in Downing Street. I went out into the street almost immediately and I can still hear the tumultuous cheering, which was repeated in Parliament, although many who cheered then would not dream of admitting it now—nor did they in 1940. In fact *The Times* and its Editor were no less 'men of Munich' than Chamberlain.

Being wise after the event is all too easy and it is a course too many have followed, including politicians and other clever boys, not only when dealing with the dark days of 1939–45 but also on such matters as the significance of Hitler in 1933, Baldwin's consequent paper on rearmament, and the aftermath of that, some of the effects of which are still with us.

I do not like the Germans, or to be more precise I hate the Huns or Prussians, and have long regretted that Julius Caesar failed in that he did not divide them, like Gaul, into a great many parts, instead of retiring to Rome with influenza to enjoy some agreeable hot baths.

The idiotic Kaiser lied to us and let us down in 1914; our treaty with Germany was torn up as a 'scrap of paper'; and even worse, perhaps, they launched poison gas against us at Ypres, ignoring the international convention which had ruled out gas as a weapon of war.

Let those who live to follow after me remember that the Germans cannot be trusted—nor can the Japs, after Pearl Harbour. They are both to be feared. People today buy Mercedes motor cars and Volkswagens because they have a reputation for good workmanship, but I for one will never knowingly buy anything made in Germany or Japan, and I hope others will on reflection take a similar view.

Perhaps the Stuarts, illegitimate or otherwise (if there be any otherwise), are more used to villainy and murder than Lord Mayors of Birmingham. Anyway, I was far from happy that night in Downing Street and, though I normally hate eating alone because company is to me a digestive, I walked alone down Birdcage Walk to Buckingham Place (not Palace) where I was living, had a solitary poached egg, and went gloomily to bed.

I was at No. 12 Downing Street when the Declaration of War became operative and I set off for the House on foot. As I approached Parliament Square some half-wit somewhere let off an air-raid 'alert' siren. I then happened to run into James Maxton, a sound fatalist, who laughed and asked in his friendly way what pacifists such as himself were supposed to do next. Many people in the street were quite rightly being told by steel-helmeted police to find the nearest shelter. Maxton and I told them we had to reach the House of Commons, and in this way we wended our way onwards, in my own case somewhat nervously. I do not know why or by whom that 'alert' was sounded, but I would have liked to strangle him. Bombing was quite bad enough when it came in earnest.

The end of Neville Chamberlain was a sad one and he did not live long after he had handed over the reins to Winston Churchill in 1940. The outcome of the debate on our withdrawal from Norway caused him to decide that he could no longer lead a War Government when it was essential to command the support of the Opposition as well as his now disunited party. Some sixty Tories had failed to support him on the Norway vote.

After Chamberlain's death, Churchill (as P.M.) said to me, 'What shall I do without poor Neville? I was relying on him to look after the Home Front for me.' The new P.M. liked and trusted his predecessor, and he was right in recognising his outstanding abilities as an administrator.

It may have been forgotten by many people now that the Minister who wound up for the Government in the Norway debate was the then First Lord of the Admiralty, Winston Churchill, and I can vouch for the fact that he put into his task every ounce of his great oratorical skill and all his energy—which in 1940 was abundant.

Immediately after the debate Chamberlain saw Lord Halifax, who did not feel that, being in the House of Lords, he was in a position to take over. Chamberlain then also saw Churchill, who accepted the great responsibility without, I have been assured, displaying any doubts about his ability to carry it, and thus the Great Wartime Coalition, as he called it, came into being. As Mr Churchill himself said to me a few years later: 'For once I did not even have to argue my own case.'

ᢟ XI ᢘ

Although I confessed at the beginning of this book that once I was a Whip I developed the ambition to be Chief Whip, I will not pretend that when I was appointed to that office my first six months were either agreeable or smooth. The simple, basic reason was that my Prime Minister did not like me and had not wanted me as successor to David Margesson, who had been sent to the War Office as Secretary of State in spite of his opposition to his own promotion. Mr Churchill and I had had what he might have called 'a little bother' in the Chamberlain days, when he was highly critical of the Government and his own Party's policy. I would prefer to call it a head-on clash, with strong words on both sides, and it was not forgotten.

Promotion in politics is by no means automatic. The fact that I was Deputy Chief Whip did not mean I would move up when Margesson moved out. Lord Fisher, the great First Sea Lord, once said that the British Empire would be wrecked if the policy of 'It's Buggins' turn' were to continue to be followed; the right man for the job might be Buggins' junior and the fact that Buggins was a very decent and popular chap should not affect the decision. The Buggins principle is certainly not adhered to in Downing Street and this, as history shows, applies to any office from Prime Minister downwards.

I am strongly anti-Buggins myself. I have told three Prime Ministers at least that they can justify any appointment provided they honestly believe that X rather than Buggins is the right man and that they can face charges of nepotism so long as the relation, be it by blood or marriage, is the best man available. I have reminded Prime Ministers of the wise remark of Campbell-Bannerman: 'You can't be a good Prime Minister unless you are a butcher.'

When Margesson went the appointment of a new Chief Whip

was urgent; but there was some delay due to disagreement at the top as to who should be chosen. As Deputy Chief Whip since 1937 it fell to me to do any essential work and to tide everything over. Certain friends who shall be nameless kept me advised as to the workings of the great minds comprising the inner circle. I made up my mind that while I was fully prepared to accept the job if it should be offered to me I had no intention of sitting on the doorstep of No. 10, lobbying or pressing my suit in any way.

I knew that the P.M. had told the War Office to bring back from the Army in the Middle East a close friend of mine, Tommy Dugdale (now Lord Crathorne) with whom I had not only worked closely in the Whips' Room immediately before the war but with whom I had been at Eton. It was the Prime Minister's intention to make him his Chief Whip and I had no desire to get in the way. I therefore went off to Scotland, leaving my address with the secretary at No. 12, the invaluable Sir Charles Harris, who from 1918 to 1957 served a variety of Chief Whips both faithfully and cheerfully.

Three or four days later I was recalled from Scotland and told to report at the War Office in the morning. I saw David, who told me that the Prime Minister intended to offer me the post. I did not learn then, owing to David's very proper discretion, how events had moved in my favour, but I did learn that there had been some quite heated arguments, running on, as was Mr Churchill's habit, into the night-watches. The main participants were, I knew, Anthony Eden (at this time our Conservative second string to Churchill), Lord Beaverbrook, Brendan Bracken (that interesting and inexplicable *éminence grise* and friend of the P.M.) and, of course, David as former Chief Whip. I gather that Eden, in the manner of Arthur Balfour, mounted the fence and took the line that 'either Dugdale or Stuart would do'. I have no doubt that Margesson backed me, while obviously the P.M., having sent for Dugdale, wanted him. Lord Beaverbrook never liked me, a feeling which was mutual, so that the balance must have rested with Brendan Bracken, whom I really did not know well at the time and whom I would never have thought, until some time later, of claiming as a friend. He was at least unbiased and always had the best interests of the Prime Minister as his main objective.

My appointment as Chief Whip—or Parliamentary Secretary to the Treasury, the official title—was announced on 15 January 1941. The P.M. had summoned me to No. 10 the previous evening, but on my arrival he was closeted with General de Gaulle. At length I was invited into the Cabinet Room where I found him in the familiar, loose 'slumber suit' of Air Force blue, designed not only for comfort but air-raid alerts, enabling him to turn out dressed at a moment's notice. Apart from the usual cigar and a glass beside him, he looked rather like a plumpish baby in toddling clothes.

He referred to the differences of opinion we had had in the past but said that times had changed and conditions with them. After a brief discourse on these lines, he offered me the post of Chief Whip. I said I regarded it as a great honour and that I would do my best to serve him and the Party.

He then talked for a time on various matters of public or national interest and importance to 'give me the background' as he put it. He referred to Lord Beaverbrook and his reliance on him, while admitting that many in the Party, and some members of the Government, were not so kindly disposed. He said he regarded Beaverbrook as a man of great energy and force and wanted him to take on more responsibilities, but that Beaverbrook was averse to this on account of his health. (Nevertheless he lived for a long time.)

The P.M. made me laugh from the very beginning, which was lucky for me, for one can't be bored or angry if one is laughing. He said, for instance, of one Member who had got into trouble at this time that 'he should join a bomb-disposal squad as the best way of rehabilitating himself in the eyes of his fellow men'—adding, after a pause, 'after all, the bombs might not go off'.

The official address of the Chief Whip is No. 12 Downing Street and from there one can walk through the hall of No. 11 (Chancellor of the Exchequer) to No. 10. One can walk on through No. 10 and over the Treasury passage (leading to the Horse Guards' Parade) through the old Treasury buildings until one's progress is blocked by the Horse Guards' arch and buildings. At this point one has to emerge and face the light of day, but when matters of top secrecy or

(a) This photograph of the author appeared in the *Daily Oklahoman* in September 1922, with the caption 'Oilfield roustabout'—when he was working in the Oklahoma oilfields.

(b) The author with his wife and eldest son, David, in 1932.

From a family group photograph taken at Christmas, 1927, at Chatsworth, home of the author's father-in-law, the 9th Duke of Devonshire. Side by side are the author and his brother-in-law by marriage, Harold Macmillan.

The sketch opposite was made by Winston Churchill during a war-time meeting at No. 10 to explain his idea for what became known as the 'kangaroo scheme'. The problem was to devise a method of sending joint messages to candidates at by-elections who were supporting the National Government. The leaders of the two sections of Liberals—Ernest Brown and Sir Archibald Sinclair—could not agree to sign together under the Prime Minister (as Leader of the Conservatives) and Mr Attlee (as Leader of the Labour Party).

Winston explained to Attlee, Sinclair and myself that he would 'carry' the Ernest Brown Liberals with the Conservatives—'like a kangaroo'. First he drew the Conservative kangaroo and then the Liberal 'baby' looking out. As he did so he said to me, 'You must see that E. B. doesn't make a mess in my pouch. I suppose the kangaroo has some strict working agreement with its young.' He then drew the Labour kangaroo, carefully pointing out to Attlee that it was not so big. As an afterthought, however, he turned up the tip of the tail, saying, 'There's no reason why I shouldn't give you a turned-up tail, Clem. After all, Labour isn't quite so down as all that.' Then he completed the drawing and said to Sinclair, 'That's you, Archie. That tiny little one at the bottom.'

The author with Winston Churchill and Lord Salisbury, 1936.

With Neville Chamberlain, 1937.

even simply discretion are involved this mode of 'invisible' progress up Whitehall has its uses. (When Anthony Eden resigned as Prime Minister in 1957, for example, I knew how to let myself in to No. 12 Downing Street, to see Harold Macmillan alone in No. 11, then to go on to see Lord Salisbury in the Lord President's office and emerge up Whitehall at a point where I would be unlikely to be seen by photographers or reporters who were extremely anxious about comings and goings in Downing Street itself. I had been in Inverness twelve hours earlier and no one, apart from Cabinet Ministers and my own office staff, knew of my activities, which was, at the time, a good thing.)

Although my life as Chief Whip was at first, like Gilbert's policeman, 'not a happy one', I managed somehow. Charles Harris, my secretary, told me later that he was afraid 'they' would 'get me down' and break me. But I had the advantage, for one thing—and I do not mean this conceitedly—that I had good personal relations over a pretty wide political field. I was on good terms with the back-benchers—and most of the Ministers— of my own Party, although by no means all of them were happy about some of the men at the top, usually because they had doubts about their past political histories.

I was something of a man in the middle, and in the interests of cohesion and stability I was kept up till any hour listening, and, if possible, explaining and 'moderating'. I sat through many trying hours of acrimonious argument, sometimes alone as the link with 'the top' and sometimes in the presence of Messrs Attlee, Eden, Beaverbrook, Ernest Bevin and, perhaps, some Minister who had got himself in the wrong and was arguing his case. I lost a lot of sleep in those years, but a Whip has to get used to that.

Clem Attlee, as Leader of the Labour Party in the Government, was always scrupulously fair and frank in all his dealings with me, as was his own Chief Whip, Will Whiteley. I got on well also with Attlee's deputy, Arthur Greenwood, until he had to leave the Government before the end of the war for reasons of health. Stafford Cripps, who joined the Cabinet on his return from Moscow as our Ambassador, was always charming to me, even when we could not agree. This may have been due in some measure to my friendship of years with his elder brother, Fred Cripps, who has written of his own roving life and whom I called 'the last of the Adventurers', just as I used to call Augustus John 'the last of the Bohemians'.

If I may be allowed one frankly immodest anecdote (I hope there are no more) I would quote a remark of Lord Attlee's, repeated to me long after the event. My informant was discussing with Attlee something he (Attlee) had written about the war days and the workings of the National Government under Churchill. My friend said, 'I suppose James Stuart had quite a lot to do with this sort of work.' 'Oh yes,' said Attlee, 'Winston could never have managed without James.' I can only plead that it would not be human to fail to derive pleasure from or to treasure such a remark.

The unexpected was almost the normal with Winston Churchill, and soon after appointing me Chief Whip he sprang an odd surprise. Having fetched Tommy Dugdale home from the Middle East for what turned out to be no purpose, he presumably felt a shade uneasy as to how to employ him. He sent for me and asked me if I could take him back into the Whips' Office as Deputy Chief Whip to myself. I replied that we were very old friends and that nothing would give me more pleasure, provided only that Tommy would consent to serve in a subordinate post.

The P.M. then asked me if I would invite him, but this was, I felt, putting too much on to me and I explained that it would be awkward for Dugdale to say 'no' to me but that he could say it to the P.M., who, after all, had engineered his return to England. The P.M. agreed and Tommy Dugdale returned to the Whips' Room where we worked as amicably as ever, and when he took over the Chairmanship of the Party at Central Office we still saw a great deal of each other and worked in close co-operation.

Before settling down in my new office I had to go through the usual preliminary tortures, such as being photographed and interviewed. I remember being asked by one journalist with a large Sunday-paper public, 'What policy do you intend to pursue in handling your back-benchers? Do you intend to follow in Margesson's footsteps?' (He had been a constant critic of my predecessor.) I answered, 'It is no use trying to out-Herod Herod,' which served well enough for the time and I knew that, if he read it, Margesson would only laugh.

In the House itself and within the Party I was treated well and fairly in all quarters. I do not pretend that I had no rows or difficulties. Every Chief Whip is bound to have both—more so, perhaps, than many Ministers, because he is dealing with so wide a variety of people and problems. But nothing in those first six months or so compared with the difficulty of my relationship with my own Leader and Prime Minister. I was in no doubt that I had been appointed against his personal wishes and he may have thought that if I did give way under strain it would merely break me and not his heart, because he could then move Tommy Dugdale up, without causing any change in the Ministerial ranks. I sincerely believe that the P.M. would not have minded if I had felt myself forced to resign or if he had felt himself able to get rid of me owing to faults or errors of judgment which could be attributed to me.

However, this did not happen and at length I received for the first time a congratulatory message from him. It was after an awkward debate in the House on the conduct of the war and the Government had a large majority. The P.M.'s message congratulated me on the size of the majority which, he said, gave him 'great satisfaction and renewed confidence in these difficult days'. I have a feeling that this personal and friendly minute may have been prompted by Brendan Bracken; its arrival was most welcome, at a time when the relationship between Churchill and myself had not yet been established on an even keel.

I had had personal messages from the P.M. before, but couched in very different terms. I shall give just one example. On one message, though it was—as usual—marked 'Urgent', it will be seen that no useful action could possibly be taken nor, in my view, would any answer have made much sense. I kept it, but I neither answered nor even acknowledged it. The Conservatives in the House had failed, in his view, to give him adequate support during a debate and the whipping boy had, of course, to be the Chief Whip. The minute demanded: 'What does the great Conservative Party think it is doing? It is like a whale stuck in the mud and unable even to flap its own tail . . .' There was more, but that gives an idea of the general tone.

But the important thing from my point of view is that from the date of that first congratulatory message quoted above our relations began to become easier and, before long, friendly. Indeed, I am pleased and proud to say that there were no further troubles in our relationship except of a very minor nature, and that even these, fortunately for my peace of mind, usually provided me with a laugh, even though sometimes at my own expense.

Winston never again failed to give me his full support and backing in the conduct of business in the House, in handling the party and, later—from 1951 until his retirement, while I served him as Secretary of State for Scotland—even when decisions and actions of mine might in other eyes have been open to criticism.

I barely knew Winston Churchill until the late 1930s and our first real encounter was, unfortunately, on a matter of disagreement. It seemed unlikely then that we would ever become close friends.

I had, of course, met him occasionally at luncheons and dinners and in other people's houses, but that was all. His period as Baldwin's Chancellor of the Exchequer (1924–9) was over some years before I became a Whip and really began to meet Ministers. Then, as a back-bencher again, he put a lot of his energies into opposing the Government over the India Bill, in which at times he had my sympathy and support. He continued through the thirties as the main critic of the Government, especially on defence and foreign policy after Hitler's rise to power. Throughout, of course, he remained a member of the Party, conducting his attacks from the sidelines, and it was this that led to our first confrontation.

The Duchess of Atholl suddenly resigned her seat as M.P. for West Perthshire in protest against the Chamberlain Government's policy. She then stood as an Independent candidate against the official Conservative. I was Scottish Whip at this time. The Duchess was, of course, very well known locally and had strong personal backing. She had done much good public work over many years and was a staunch supporter of many good causes. But we too had a good local candidate in William McNair Snadden, a successful and popular Perthshire farmer. He held the seat for the Party satisfactorily (and became, much later, one of my Under-Secretaries in the Scottish Office) but it was an anxious period, made even more worrying for me when Mr Churchill sent the Duchess a telegram of encouragement, although he was a member of the Party she was fighting! I fear that this incident led to some harsh words, perhaps mostly on my part, and the wound took a long time to heal.

No one will deny that Winston Churchill was a great man, but only history will value him at his proper worth. I heard him say in the House once, in reply to a questioner who was pressing him for further details on some awkward point, 'Only history can relate the full story'; and then he added, after exactly the right pause, 'And I shall write the history.'

He has written his story of the two World Wars and much has been written about him, so I propose to confine myself, in writing of him, to personal experience and some incidents and stories that I have not seen recorded before.

He was not an easy man to work with or to serve: far from it. He was argumentative; he wanted his own way (but who does not?) and he was a bit of a bully. He was not an intellectual and never claimed to be a scholar. His knowledge of the classics, of foreign languages, even of arithmetic, was negligible, but his interest and feeling for history was deep and wide, especially with regard to that of—in the widest sense—his fellow countrymen, as was amply demonstrated by what proved to be his last publication, his *History of the English-speaking Peoples*.

He was probably the greatest war-time leader the British have ever known, but had it not been for the 1939-45 war I am convinced he would never have become Prime Minister. In the year when he succeeded Neville Chamberlain—1940—he was sixty-five, a fact worth bearing in mind because it is the age at which a man can draw the Old Age Pension (and five years older than the pensionable age for women!). The vigour with which he assumed, at this advanced age, the vast responsibilities and unrelenting pressures of the highest office in the land, and kept it up for more than five years of war, has become part of history.

Concentration was one of the keys to his character. It was not always obvious, but he never really thought of anything but the job in hand. He was not a fast worker, especially when dealing with papers, but he was essentially a non-stop worker. I do not mean that he did not rest; he was too wise for that. But perhaps I can best illustrate what I mean this way: when he was painting in his studio at Chartwell he would stand back from his current canvas, pull at his cigar, and contemplate the picture for a while. Then he would approach it and make a brush stroke or two, after which he would retreat to his chair, puff his cigar and perhaps sip a whisky and soda, still staring hard at the canvas. Then he would suddenly say to me, 'I am very worried about the attitude of our Labour colleagues to the Trade Disputes Act. I wonder what would be the wise course to adopt . . .' and so on.

His power of application at any time of day or night was phenomenal, while his hours of work were, of course, so unusual as to be unique, unless it be true that Napoleon's were comparable. As an example, he telephoned me once, in the middle of the war, at 8.30 a.m. in a hot temper to ask whether I had read a certain newspaper. I said I was sorry but that I had not yet had time. He replied, 'Well, you ought to have had. Get it and read it and be with me at 9.30.' I hurried and did my best but there were no taxis in sight anywhere and I had a walk of about a mile. On arrival at Storey's Gate—our war H.Q.—a Secretary told me that the P.M. had gone to sleep again but would see me in twenty minutes. I was duly summoned and there was the Great Man in bed: wide awake now, he swiftly re-lost his temper and went for me as though I had some responsibility for publishing this attack on the Government. Some weeks later, when I was alone with him and work was over for the night, I ventured to remark to him how astounded I was that anyone could lose his temper, almost immediately thereafter go to sleep again for twenty minutes, and then wake up and lose his temper all over again. The calm reply was, 'Ah, you must understand—if I am not asleep within three of four minutes of packing it up, then something must be very wrong.' And this remarkable habit persisted throughout my years with him.

I have just used the words 'great' and 'remarkable' and these were the same two words used of him by Edward Wood, the late Lord Halifax, who had worked with him and who was Foreign Secretary when he became P.M. I visited Edward at Garrowby, his home in Yorkshire, shortly before his death and almost at once he said, 'Tell me, James, how is that great and remarkable man, Winston?' The significance of this lies in the difference between the two men. Halifax and Churchill had nothing in common and it is impossible to imagine them matched in harness.

Churchill too had the quality of being able to admire people utterly unlike himself. Neville Chamberlain is a perfect example;

Winston recognised his clarity of thought, brevity of expression and ability to concentrate on essentials while ruthlessly jettisoning the dead wood.

I always admired the fact that Winston appeared to me to be thinking at least thirty years ahead. Strangely enough, he greatly admired this quality in others—and in one (to me) very surprising case in particular. He had a great friend in the late Duke of Westminster (known as 'Bendor') with whom he used to dine quite often, even in the war when he seldom went out to a meal at all. I couldn't help asking him once why he usually accepted the Duke's invitations but seldom any others. 'Bendor', he said, 'is one of my oldest friends. If he had not been a Duke, he would have got the V.C. in the First War. He is incapable of expressing himself but he is always thinking a hundred years ahead.'

Winston himself would sometimes raise subjects surprisingly remote from the matters in hand. For instance I have a 'Personal Minute' dated 18 March 1945—that is, before the end of the war in the West, far less the war against Japan—which reads as follows:

CHIEF WHIP

Look up the Motion or Bill moved about 1888 by Curzon, Brodrick, and Wolmer asking for relief from going to the Lords on their fathers' decease.

It is a terrible thing for a father to doom his son to political extinction, which must happen to many if they have not had time to make their way in the House of Commons.

WSC

This reached me out of the blue; the subject had not been mentioned before. Yet what Winston was thinking about then, in the midst of his vast responsibilities, became an important issue several years later and was resolved only by the legislation which enabled Sir Alec Douglas-Home and Quintin Hogg (to name only two) to give up their titles and return to the House of Commons to play far more significant roles than they had been able to do as hereditary peers.

I always feel that printed stories of Churchill are inadequate; he was inimitable (though far too many imitators have tried) and the mannerisms were part of him—his slight hesitation in pronunciation, for example, or the way in which he emphasised certain words. He was an English purist and hated words derived from foreign sources. He once said to me (as a Scotsman) 'Mayn't I *ever* be allowed to use the word *England*? Must I always say *Britain* or *British*? I *like* England.'

He corrected me on numerous occasions on my use or choice of words: for example, I was not allowed to say 'aerodrome'; only airfield or airport was permitted. And he was quite angry when I referred to Nelson's family's home near Salisbury as 'Trăfălgăr'; he insisted on 'Trăfālgăr'. I explained that my pronunciation was nearer to the name of the Cape and was used normally in Wiltshire. His reply, uttered in no uncertain terms, was, 'Never mind that, it's not *English.*'

He asked me once why the Foreign Office insisted on using the word 'viable' and what did they mean? Of course he knew perfectly well, so I simply said that it was a French term meaning something like 'capable of life' or 'of existence'. 'Well, why don't they say so?' was his comment.

I know that this next anecdote has been recounted—and distorted—before, but it happened in my presence. When Winston was going through a Foreign Office statement which Anthony Eden, as Foreign Secretary, wanted him to approve for publication, he pulled out his red-ink pen and said to me, 'Typical Foreign Office verbiage. It contains every cliché except "Please adjust your dress before leaving".'

No man was quicker or better at improving a brief put before him. He didn't tear it up or re-write it but improved and shortened it with a few red-ink strokes without affecting the meaning. To be given a rough draft of a letter or statement was what he liked: it saved him the trouble of starting from zero and he could then knock it into shape very quickly.

He once asked me to draft a letter for him to be read in the House of Lords in secret session at the end of the war, to thank the Lords for the use of their Chamber after we had been bombed and burnt out of the Commons in May 1941. It was a laborious task and I put some hours of work into it. The result ran to three pages of typewriting. A couple of days later I was sent for from my adjacent office at No. 12 Downing Street. The P.M.'s principal secretary, Leslie Rowan (now Sir Leslie and Managing Director of Vickers) was on duty and as I arrived I said to him, 'What's the trouble now?' 'Nothing's the trouble,' he replied. 'All's well and you're the blue-eyed boy. You have achieved the impossible.'

He then explained that for the first time in the experience of both of us the Old Man had approved a draft letter without altering even a comma. 'Go right on in,' said Leslie. 'He wants to see you.'

Winston was sitting as usual at the Cabinet table, glaring at his papers and chewing the inevitable cigar. He had my letter beside him, properly typed and ready for signature. 'Did you write this yourself?' he demanded. I replied, 'Yes, Prime Minister, as a matter of fact I did.' 'It is very good,' he said, 'I will sign it.' After he had done so, and since he was in one of his benign moods, I could not resist saying, 'If you had criticised my choice of words I had my answer all ready in advance, but now I needn't use it. I took every adjective and most of the nouns out of your own writings and speeches.'

A tiny example of how Winston could deal swiftly and succinctly with questions put to him is typified in one of the few pieces of paper I happen to have preserved. The time was mid-war and the subject of the debate does not matter now, but I wrote: 'Should the Minister of Labour be asked to be present during the debate on Thursday and be prepared to wind it up if necessary?' In blunt red pencil beneath this are the words 'No, sir'. Perhaps it is also typical that when the time came the Minister (Ernest Bevin) *did* wind up the debate.

Churchill stories chase each other through my head. So many have never been recorded and I am writing from memory as I never kept diaries. I wish men like Lord Ismay and Lord Chandos in their admirable books had told more of them (and Lord Moran fewer, but that is another matter); and unless Brendan Bracken, who was probably closer to Churchill than anyone, left anecdotes among his papers when he died, many more will have been lost to us.

It is perhaps appropriate here to digress briefly on Lord Moran's unexpected butting into the political history of the last twenty-five years of Churchill's life with his very long book* commenting on events not confined to Sir Winston's pulse or temperature and largely well outside what I would have thought to be the concern of a medical adviser.

I saw Lord Moran at times in Downing Street or elsewhere as he came and went about his professional business while others, including myself, came and went on our own quite different business. None of us ever imagined that this dedicated doctor was in any way concerned with the conduct of the war or with our political affairs.

Apart from saying 'Good morning', or similar conventional exchanges, I never entered into any conversation with him since his job was one of which I had no sort of knowledge. My conversation might well have bored him—or his me. Randolph Churchill was right when he wrote (in the *Daily Telegraph*) that Lord Moran did not see the Churchill family at any time when all was well and no anxiety regarding health existed. If there was occasion for worry, the doctor was called, of course; he therefore saw Sir Winston only when his health was threatened, when he would take his pulse or whatever else was called for, including calling in other doctors and specialists as required. One naturally talks to one's doctor when confined to bed—*faute de mieux*—and may talk of matters of a highly confidential nature, but it has to be remembered that so long as normal good health prevailed Sir Winston pursued his endless labours and controlled his Ministers effectively, and there was no thought on our part that he failed in any way to perform his Herculean task.

The time comes, of course, in the lives of all men when deterioration, mental or physical or both, begins to manifest itself, and there is no fixed age at which the decline begins. Sir Winston withstood advancing years in a manner which must be almost unprecedented, but no man can pretend to be totally unaffected after, say, his fifties. Most people begin to forget names or faces, while young soldiers and policemen appear to be mere boys.

I can remember Winston, while composing a speech when he

*Winston Churchill: *The Struggle for Survival 1940–65* (Constable).

was in his seventies, saying to me, 'The ideas are all there'—
pointing to the ceiling—'but I find it more difficult now to get
them down on to paper.' But he did get them down in due course
and was always ready to deliver the speech at the right time up to
the day of his retirement.

One of my favourite Churchill stories dates back to his Treasury
days in the twenties. He had made a slight slip during the Committee stage of one of his Finance Bills but had agreed that he must
restore the position later, during the Report stage: that is to say,
he had to persuade the House to reverse its decision in Committee
by restoring a clause to its original, or Second Reading, form.

His principal secretary at the time was that highly intelligent
and able civil servant, P. J. Grigg (later Sir James Grigg and
Secretary of State for War). On the morning of the day when the
clause was to come before the House again, P. J. brought Churchill
his papers saying, '. . . and you will remember, Chancellor, that
you have to restore the position on Clause X, but it's not of great
importance and I don't think you need make heavy weather of
it.'

The Chancellor, eyeing him, replied, 'I think I know more about
the Parl. (sic) than you do. I have thought about it and I intend
to adopt the high moral tone, 'you be b—, and all that.'

During the days of Churchill's opposition to the India Bill,
Patrick Buchan-Hepburn (now Lord Hailes) was acting as an
unpaid private secretary to Churchill and they were having trouble
over drafting an amendment—always a difficult job. Neither was
satisfied with the draft when Winston, the realist, rose from the
table to go to lunch, saying that the wording was good enough
and would have to do. Patrick replied conscientiously that surely
Mr Churchill would not table an amendment unless and until he
was satisfied that he had got it into precisely the right form.
Churchill turned at the door and said, 'Young man, you should
have been a clergyman.'

Jumping ahead to my time at the Scottish Office, I recall being
asked, at a Conservative Club in Scotland, to tell the company my
favourite story about the P.M., who had just retired from office.
I was taken by surprise, but the story that came to my mind was of

Winston's visit to Greece during the war, with the Service Chiefs and others, when a decision had to be reached as to who should command the Greek forces. I was not present but I was told on good authority that when the decisive meeting took place, on a very hot afternoon on board one of H.M. ships, the argument dragged on and on but it appeared that a Greek general named Plastiras was gaining most backing. The P.M., anxious to wind up the meeting, pronounced, 'Very well, gentlemen, it would appear that you are ready to put your faith in General Plaster-arse. Let us hope that his feet are not of clay.'

When, in the same discussions, the matter in hand was the political set-up, a certain prelate of the Greek Church seemed to be favoured and after a while the P.M. turned to our commander on the spot, a young Scots brigadier, and asked his view. The brigadier was not used to Winstonian methods or conversation, nor did he regard this wholly political problem as coming within the terms of his command. However, he went so far as to say that this particular candidate did appear to be as competent to run some sort of government as anyone else available.

The P.M. pressed the brigadier further. 'Tell me, General,' he asked, 'Would you regard this prelate as an artful, scheming priest?' To this the startled soldier, while not having contemplated such a description, admitted that one might describe him in such terms. This was good enough for Winston, who wound up the business by saying, 'Good. Then that's our man.'

The P.M. would argue hotly and constantly in favour of his own view and often consumed much time in doing so. He enjoyed arguments and sitting up late, but if one had a good case to put against him he would come round and alter his view, even though his closest friends like Brendan Bracken or Beaverbrook had supported him in his earlier line.

Quite early in my time with him, in 1941, he had sent Brendan to the Ministry of Information and wanted a new Parliamentary Private Secretary. He sent for me as Chief Whip and as I approached his room I met Brendan in the passage. He asked me what I had come to do. I told him, to which he replied that I need not bother because he had already fixed it with 'the Boss'. I asked who it was and his answer disturbed me, because I regarded his nominee as being most unsuited and not tough enough for the job. However, I merely said that, having been sent for, I had better go in.

The P.M. told me what he had agreed with Bracken, adding, 'You see, I must have someone to keep the flies off me.' By a happy chance I answered straight off the cuff, 'But, good heavens, you have chosen a bluebottle.' Curiously, he never even argued the matter, but appointed my man, George Harvie-Watt, so I won by good luck rather than clever management.

Churchill was at his best when things were worst. I was a ready audience and, fortunately, well practised in sitting up late. The loss of sleep was worth it for his talk, and even when he was, in the main, dealing with very serious subjects, there was always a moment when he slipped in some comment that made me laugh.

I remember telling him that a certain M.P. (well within service age) had at last gone into the R.A.F.—to do a ground job with the rank of flight lieutenant. 'I know,' said Winston. 'More flight than lieutenant about him.'

In a debate in the House about this time the late Lord Winterton had complained that the Government had not made full use of their opportunities. He was good enough to say that they had 'not been days of lead, neither had they been golden'. He preferred to call them 'silver-gilt'. Churchill whispered to me on the Bench, 'I suppose the next book will be *The Silver-Guilty Men*'—an allusion to a scurrilous book attacking the Chamberlain Government, entitled *Guilty Men* and written under the pseudonym of 'Cato'.

In an argument with him about the best way to conduct some debate, Herbert Morrison (then Home Secretary) and I were in agreement, and we eventually prevailed. I then said to Winston that I was sorry if I had misunderstood him in the first place. He put his hand on my arm at once saying, 'My dear, that's quite all right.' He never uttered a word of complaint and I remarked to Herbert as we left that I didn't mind offering an apology provided one got one's way. I think that in many matters Winston provoked argument—sometimes heated—as the best way of educating himself and reaching the right conclusion.

Visiting him one morning in the annexe at Storey's Gate I found him in bed naked, just having been massaged. He said, 'I must apologise for my costume. I was being rubbed.' I said I did not see any costume. 'Why?' he demanded. 'What's wrong with my birthday suit?' Just to make it more bizarre, he was smoking a cigar at the time.

Early in 1942 the P.M. suddenly decided that some Ministerial changes must be made. He asked me whether we had 'any good dukes'. 'All must be engaged in this struggle,' he said. 'Proletariat and Peers—and I shall rub their noses together.' His ability to surprise one was unfailing.

Looking back, I realise that we all had our different methods of handling this unusual man. Harold Macmillan and Oliver Lyttelton (Lord Chandos) would amuse him by their conversational wit; David Maxwell Fyfe (now Lord Kilmuir) would argue earnestly with all his heart and conviction. Sir John Dill (Chief of the Imperial Staff and a man of great ability) would state his military views quietly and sincerely, but prolonged argument tired him. Dill was, if anything, almost too nice for dealing with some of those he had to convince and win over to his side. Churchill in private talk referred to him as 'the family solicitor'.

Field-Marshal Sir Alan Brooke (the late Lord Alanbrooke), who succeeded Dill, shot back at the P.M.'s arguments like a burst of machine-gun fire, but I felt he wasted both breath and mental energy at times. It was a constant practice of the P.M. to try out his latest brainwave on the Chiefs of Staff and others and to await their reactions, but Alan Brooke—a first-class soldier and staff officer—did not always think it funny.

It is said that, after the Norway misadventure, Admiral of the Fleet Lord Cork and Orrery—that tough and forceful sailor known in the Navy as 'Ginger Boyle'—kept on pestering the Admiralty and Downing Street weekly, if not daily, to give him another command. Admirals of the fleet, like field-marshals and presumably air chief marshals, are always on the active list. One day the P.M. was in his Map Room, down on his hands and knees studying an enormous map laid out for him on the floor. He had beside him a naval officer to answer questions. Somewhere up at the top, or northern, end of this map, the P.M.'s attention was distracted by a mark of some sort. Thinking it was his own cigar ash, he tried to blow it away, but without result; then, moving closer, he swept at it with his coat cuff, but again with no result. Irritated, he said to the officer, 'What's that smudge up there?' 'That, sir,' came the reply, 'is the Shetland Islands.' 'Well then,' said the P.M., 'send Lord Cork to defend them.'

And there the admiral went—to the annoyance of the local islanders, whose roads and bridges he is said to have mined against invasion.

Two incidents which demonstrate Brendan Bracken's unique relationship with Churchill amused me greatly and on both occasions I was the only other person present. It must be remembered that Brendan had the entrée at almost any time.

It was one o'clock in the morning, or later, and we were in the P.M.'s sitting-room at Storey's Gate. We had finished work, having dealt with the answers to his Questions in the House for the following day. He sat in his flowered Chinese silk dressing-gown beside the fire, the usual cigar in his mouth, but he was tired and was relaxing, his eyes more or less closed. Brendan entered without warning, stuck a cigarette in his mouth and looked round for matches but saw none. Not a word had been spoken; he walked up to the P.M.'s armchair and, leaning forward with a hand on each arm, he lit his cigarette from the cigar end. The P.M. never looked up and said no word to Brendan but, turning his head towards me, remarked, 'I have murdered men for less than that.'

I should add that he hated the smell of cigarettes anyway and constantly forced a cigar on me to prevent me smoking cigarettes.

The other incident was during a week-end at Ditchley, near Oxford, where Ronald Tree, M.P., lived at that time and where the P.M. was advised to go at times to ring the changes from Chequers in order to avoid bombing. I was alone with the P.M. after dinner discussing a Ministerial appointment, since I felt strongly that his man was not the right one for the particular post which had soon to be filled. During our talk Brendan Bracken drifted into the room at the far end and Winston called, 'I want you, Brendan.' He then told B.B. the position and named the possible candidates for the post, indicating his own preference. It so happened that the P.M.'s choice was, like himself, an old Harrovian. Schools had, of course, not been mentioned but the P.M. knew I was an Etonian. Bracken was neither. To my surprise, pleasure, and amusement, Brendan's immediate reply to the P.M. was, 'I agree with the Chief Whip. You only want X because he was at that bloody old Borstal of yours. I hope to God it won't be going "forty years on".'

Winston merely turned to me and said quietly, 'He's very unkind, isn't he?'

I have already referred to the Scottish habit of saying it is about time for a 'small refreshment'—mysterious to foreigners such as Englishmen, but meaning simply a double whisky. It has been said of Churchill that as a younger man he was in the habit of using drink rather liberally, but I knew only of his later years (after the age of sixty-five) when his intake was certainly not excessive. He liked to have a drink beside him and he would sip it occasionally; one small whisky and soda would last him for three-quarters of an hour. He used to balance his cigar across the top of the tumbler between puffs and in Cabinet he liked to have a large tumbler of iced soda water beside him, and balance the cigar on that.

The whole subject of drinking is apt to arouse strong feelings in the breasts of the 'unco guid' so I shall say at once that I resort to refreshment of a stimulating type, whether small or large, at all sorts of hours, and looking back to the First World War days in France and Belgium I have often thought that I could not have survived the wet and the mud without its reviving effect. Being under twenty-one, I did not, of course, need much to achieve the required result, but there is little doubt that the First World War caused me to absorb more at an earlier age than I would have in times of peace.

Winston Churchill told me once that he had never drunk whisky before he went to India as a young officer with the 4th Hussars. Normally he liked champagne and brandy, but in India the transport of whisky was simpler, so it became the normal beverage. I remember also that in one of his writings, referring to his Army service in France with the Grenadiers, he tells how he found himself forced to arrange to be removed from Battalion Headquarters to a company in the front line. He proceeds to explain that he does not want the reader to think that his reason for this move was any excess of martial valour, or words to that effect. The point was that his commanding officer, Colonel Jeffreys (General Lord Jeffreys) used no beverage stronger than strong tea.

I remember having lunch with him at Chartwell once when he wanted to see me about some changes in the organisation of the Unionist Party in Scotland, of which he had made me Chairman. It was a hot morning and we had champagne for lunch. I had sat up in a train all night and I said something about being tired and how good it was to see champagne, which didn't often come my way for lunch. 'But you see how much simpler it is,' he said, 'I buy only champagne, so when I say to my butler "Bring some more wine" he can't go wrong because there's nothing else to bring!' I congratulated him on this labour-saving device.

Later in the day, Mrs Churchill came into the room where we were working and said we were late for tea; did we want any? Winston asked me and I shook my head. He then turned to her saying 'No, thank you,' and added 'but send us a little whisky and soda', then looking up at her and grinning like a naughty boy he added, 'I admit I have had a little already.'

His appetite was remarkable and he could, I think, digest practically anything; I doubt whether he knew the meaning of the word indigestion. I remember at dinner, when he was in his mid-eighties, having some excellent soup followed by sole and half a grouse: this was more than adequate for me and I was labouring when some sort of pudding appeared, at which stage I asked to be excused because I could eat no more. Lady Churchill said that she understood perfectly, but that she simply had to lay on these big meals every day. She added that she had recently had strawberries and cream for dinner and that Winston looked at them and said, 'Where's my pudding?' She explained that strawberries were then at their best and that she knew he liked them. He did not contradict her but merely reiterated, 'Yes, but I haven't had my pudding.'

He was very fond of good clear soup which, he often said to me, was so refreshing if one was tired. He would not touch thick soups. Once at about 2 a.m. in the House of Commons, when business had detained us, he said he wanted some clear soup. I explained that the kitchens were closed but that I could get him an egg and bacon in the Dining Room or some Bovril in the Tea Room. I don't think he had ever heard of a Tea Room, so I advised that he should follow me. Cigar in mouth and whisky and soda in hand he did so, but as we entered the Tea Room I said, 'I am afraid you can't smoke here.' This caused an immediate rebellious reaction and he asked me who had said so. I pointed to a notice on the wall which said 'No Smoking. By order of the Kitchen Committee.' After glowering at it, he growled, 'There's no law against it,' and, sitting down, went on with his cigar.

He seldom troubled to carry any money with him but the Smoking Room stewards, contrary to another unwritten law, kept his bar account, which he paid periodically when he remembered to bring some money. Once I was with him when the steward told him how much he owed and he produced two or three £1 notes. This was soon after the Labour Party got their big majority in 1945 and they had decided to tidy up some of our bad habits. Among the changes the Kitchen Committee had decided that tipping should be abolished. Instead, a black tin box had been placed near the bar and one could insert coins to help swell the funds of the staff's summer outing. I told Winston this and got the usual irritated rejoinder, telling me, as I knew, that there was no *law* against tipping. When the steward returned with the change, amounting to several shillings, Winston waved it away and whispered behind his hand, very loudly, 'You keep that—and pay no attention to that damned box.'

Winston was always a most generous man and a most generous host. He never allowed one to pay for anything in his company, except on the not unusual occasions when he had no money with him and had to pay a taxi or tip a hall porter.

He could be tough and even resort to bullying if need be, but he was kind and forgiving at the end of the day to all whom he liked or trusted. Early in my days as Chief Whip he had to get rid of two highly-placed Ministers, always a worrying operation. I said that, while we were at it, he might as well get rid of a third, on the grounds that it was better to get it over in one massacre because the Press would not then be able to concentrate all their attention on one victim—that is to say, criticism would be divided by three. I quoted again the Campbell-Bannerman saying about a P.M. having to be a butcher.

He agreed after some argument but he came down to dinner at Chequers in a very depressed and almost lugubrious mood. The two ladies beside him made suitable noises expressing sympathy and trying to help with words to the effect that his task must be well-nigh unbearable. They can have had no more than a vague idea of what was afoot, but after a few minutes and a glass of wine diluted by his tears Winston came back to his normal, naughty self and, looking up, saw me down the table. He raised his hand and, pointing at me, shouted, 'He is the butcher. He told me to do it.' The others were mystified and the secretaries laughed because he had contrived to put me in the wrong.

However, I got back at him two or three weeks later when I told him that the silly man Z, of whom we had got rid, had sent a spy (a silly M.P.) to see me and ask why Z had been shelved. The P.M. asked me how I had handled this, to which I was glad to be able to answer that I could give no explanation as it was none of my business. 'But', said Winston, 'you told me to sack him.' I agreed, but added that it was his task to appoint or dismiss Ministers, with the monarch's consent, and that it was not within my area of responsibilities.

❧ XIII ❧

Looking back, I fear that I may have given the impression that it was all great fun and that it was easy to handle the man who was our war-time Prime Minister and Leader of the Opposition from 1945 to 1951. If so, I have done wrong, for he was without doubt one of the most difficult men imaginable to deal with.

Throughout my years with him, I never ceased to be disturbed and worried—to the point where it affected my internal workings—whenever I was sent for unexpectedly and without previous knowledge of what was in his mind. It might be education—not my strong subject; or it might be the fact that the apes on the rock of Gibraltar were in danger of dying out, a sure sign, if not prevented, that the end of the British Empire was upon us and that action must be taken 'this day'.

He kept a packet of printed labels beside him bearing the words —'Immediate: Action this day'. These he personally stuck on all sorts of memoranda which he dictated and dispatched to Ministers or Chiefs of Staff after initialling and dating them in his own hand. He insisted, very rightly, on dating any document to which he subscribed his signature or initials. Some of these memoranda carried the imprint of genius; many were funny—intentionally or otherwise—while some were just impossible.

Fred Leathers (Lord Leathers) as Minister of Transport was, in his early days, not quite used to his chief's methods, and was at moments in doubt as to how to deal with the commands which arrived at his Ministry. It had, for example, been agreed at a high level that during the war all new road development and improvement works must cease as being not essential for the war effort. There were, however, three exceptions where completion was of great importance and of these the Uxbridge by-pass, vital to the R.A.F., had to be pushed on.

One week-end the P.M. was being driven from London to

Chequers and, as was his custom, he had a little sleep, but, as always, he had beside him one of his 'young ladies' (as he called the members of the Downing Street secretariat). At the end of the new road there was a traffic hold-up due to the linking up of the new by-pass with the main Oxford road. The halt awoke the P.M. He was told that the delay was due to the new road work. This annoyed him, though it is true he was not aware of the important nature of the work. Turning to the secretary, he said with some irritation, 'Take this down: "Minister of Transport. I was delayed on my journey to Chequers owing to some new road works. Are you not aware that there is a war on? Pray cease this fooling".'

It was during his periods of relaxation, usually after work late at night, that he was at his best and turned on the charm, which he could do with huge success. I was seeing him to bed at Chartwell late one night, after an unexpected journey from the North, when he turned it on suddenly and said he was afraid that he had often given me a lot of trouble. Work being over and bed close at hand, I told him not to worry and that anyway it interested me. I then started to say something but faltered, adding, 'No, I won't say that; it might annoy you.' He patted my arm two or three times saying, 'Go on. Tell, tell, tell.' I then said I would, provided that he promised not to lose his temper. He promised, so I told him that he reminded me of the man whose mistress said of him that he 'sometimes was a headache but never was a bore'. He said, 'Do you mean that?' I answered that I did, truthfully. His response was, 'Thank you so much, my dear,' and then, in his night attire, he insisted on escorting me to my room, although I already knew quite well where it was. Finding his cat in the passage he bent down to stroke it, saying, 'Darling, you have been very unkind to me; you haven't been near me all day.'

This cat would get on his bed and curl up to sleep in one of his open official red boxes and when I tried to find the letter or paper he wanted to discuss he would say, 'I do wish you'd find the right papers—but don't disturb the cat'—not easy if the cat happened to be lying on it.

When he worked in bed, as he so often did, he had a bed-table the legs of which reached down to the floor on each side of the bed, so that it remained steady while he could move about underneath. Over his elbows he applied covers made of some sort of Dunlopillo to avoid discomfort, and by his bedside stood a lighted candle in a silver candlestick from which he would light his cigar. With all this, and the cat and a fire blazing in a hermetically sealed bedroom, the great man produced a magnificent spectacle—though one could often hardly breathe for lack of air.

During my years as Chief Whip, whether in office or in Opposition, I had to attend all the vast Party conferences, which entailed visits for two or three nights to such places as Blackpool, Brighton, Edinburgh, Glasgow and Ayr. On the day of Churchill's big speech at Ayr, during one of the Scottish conferences, we lunched in his sitting-room at the Station Hotel with only one other person present—Sir Alexander Walker, head of the famous whisky firm based on Kilmarnock and 'still going strong'. Churchill had a high opinion of Walker's abilities.

During lunch, Walker asked his host who was likely to succeed him in the Party leadership, adding, 'I can't see the man with the fire in his belly for the job.' He got no direct answer to this but the words 'fire in his belly' gave me an idea, which, however, I could not voice; yet the same thought had not escaped Churchill, because a few minutes later, as Walker was preparing to depart, I heard him say, 'By the way, you know what you said about a man with fire in his belly? Well, if I was short at any time, do you think you could help me out with a little whisky?' Whisky was still one of our many shortages and 'Johnnie Walker' was a favourite of Churchill's.

When his guests had gone Winston returned to work on his speech for the big meeting that evening. When this was finished, I left him to get some air while he had a rest. When I returned to his room, with only eight minutes in hand before we were due to leave the hotel, I found him in his shirt but trouserless. I exclaimed that he was due on the platform in about ten minutes and that he would be late, upon which he rounded on me, saying, 'I have never been late for a public engagement yet.' (This may have been true up to a point, but I have known of trains which have waited for him: on that same trip, the night train from

London had to wait at Kilmarnock while he got his clothes on, with the Provost and other dignitaries all lined up and waiting on the platform to greet him.)

But that evening in Ayr we got to the meeting in reasonable time and the platform party had started towards their seats when I heard a plaintive voice behind me, like a hurt and helpless child, saying, 'James, James, I can't make a speech. I've left my glasses behind.' I knew they must be in his hotel room, so I told him not to worry and that I would run and get them. I also said I would tell the organist to go on playing 'Land of Hope and Glory' (which he loved and usually made him cry) until I got back.

Luckily the hotel was only three minutes away and his detective, who was younger than I, did the run. The spectacles were found and the upset child became the great man again.

At the end of the meeting the organ blared forth again with 'Land of Hope and Glory' and 'For He's a Jolly Good Fellow'— but then, not according to plan, the audience started up spontaneously with 'Will ye no' come back again'. Churchill stopped as he was leaving the platform and turning to me said, 'That's a lovely song.' 'Yes,' I said, 'Jacobite.' This got him off the platform, his family's sympathies having been Hanoverian while mine were obviously Stuart.

Colonel P. J. Blair, D.S.O., who ran our Party office in Scotland and did everything to help me during my thirty-five years of political life, said to me as he followed us out that we were 'like two little children bickering'. But it was a hot evening and after a long speech I was thirsty and, of course, very anxious for 'a small refreshment'.

On the subject of more solid refreshment I am not alone in having been surprised at Churchill's capacity. At one Blackpool conference I was in his bedroom at 9.30 a.m., helping in any way I could with the preparation of his speech for the following afternoon. There was a knock on the door and the hotel manager entered to inquire about his distinguished guest's requirements for dinner. This was about the only type of interruption he would tolerate while at work; he even welcomed it. The manager suggested, *inter alia*, oysters and roast grouse, both of which had Churchill's immediate agreement. He was preparing to get down to his dictation again as the manager left, but he suddenly looked up and shouted after the man. I hurried into the passage and retrieved him, wondering what on earth could have happened in thirty seconds of peace engendered by the comforting thought of oysters, grouse, and champagne.

He looked up at the manager leaning over the bed and said simply, 'Oysters on the deep shell, of course', and so back to work.

The dinner was good and all went very well; at the end the manager asked if all had been to Mr Churchill's liking. He received the desired assurance and was about to move on when he was halted again. 'By the way,' said Mr C., 'we didn't finish all the grouse, did we?' 'Oh, no,' said the manager. 'Then', said Winston, 'do you think you could let me have half a cold grouse with my breakfast in the morning?' 'Certainly,' replied the manager, adding, 'You mean instead of eggs and bacon?' 'No,' came the immediate reply, 'I mean *after* my eggs and bacon.'

After dinner that night, five of us retired to a sitting-room to discuss the day's doings at the conference. The Leader of the Conservative Party does not attend the conferences but winds up at the end of the last day with a lengthy and all-embracing speech covering foreign, domestic and economic affairs. The other three present that night, who came to report how the various resolutions had been dealt with, were Anthony Eden, David Maxwell Fyfe, and Oliver Stanley, whose death in the late forties caused so much sorrow, as he would have attained high office. These three advised Mr C. that he really ought to write into his speech for the next day a few paragraphs dealing in an arresting way with our Party's view on the future, concentrating in particular on the great part to be played by youth.

After a bit of such talk, Winston told the three of them to go over to a table in the corner and write down briefly what they thought he should say. While they went to work, he suggested that he and I should relax with a little whisky and soda. When we had settled down in the most distant corner he pointed to their backs, remarking gleefully to me, 'Isn't this a good idea? They can do the work while we have a little drink.'

It was about 3 a.m. when we got to bed. I was at his bedside by 9.30 a.m. and I found him already at work, aided by the inevitable cigar and a lighted candle. I ventured to ask him what he intended to do with the material provided by our friends the previous night, and how he liked it. His reply was that it was lying on the floor somewhere and that he hadn't had time to think about all these new brainwaves. The interesting thing to me was that, in the end, he made his own speech in his own way and never even bothered to explain to the others why he had totally ignored their views, nor did they refer to the matter. He was tough enough to follow his own line without being led aside by novel views wished on him by others (even when invited) and he was big enough to discard without explanation or apology material he did not relish. Of course he was well aware of the fact that he himself was better able than anyone else alive to make a hit on the platform: the greater the audience and the louder the organ, the more lively the speech.

I referred earlier to our occasional friendly bickerings about the rival merits of the Stuarts and the Hanoverians. When Winston had more or less completed *The English-speaking Peoples* he asked me to read what he had written about Prince Charles Edward Stuart and the 1745 rising, and to let him have my comments.

I read it with interest and wrote to him from my family's house in Moray. I said that I was writing from a room looking out towards a road, less than a mile and a half away, along which the Prince's army had marched from Kinloss to Nairn, and then on to Culloden the following day, where they were faced with the Duke of Cumberland and his army a day later. I explained frankly that my family had not participated, believing it to be a lost cause without French troops and money.

I added that I was glad to note that he too disliked Cromwell, but that his dislike could not be greater than mine because my family had been fined 3,000 guineas on account of their Stuart sympathies. I concluded by expressing relief that, according to our records, we had not paid much more than half of the fine before the Restoration relieved us.

The Churchillian reply, which gave me great pleasure, was typical:

116

at La Pausa,
Roquebrune-Cap Martin, A.M.
17 January 1958

My dear James,

I have just reached here and your letter catches me up. Here for the moment we have delicious sunshine, which I value greatly. Heath* told me I could go away, which was very kind of him. Do your wayward steps ever lead you to the Riviera? If so, let me know.

Your reminiscences of the '45 are very interesting. I am sure you would have had your head cut off.

Yours ever,
WINSTON CHURCHILL

Although there is no rule against it, the maiden speech of a new M.P. is normally not bellicose or highly controversial: the House listens quietly and congratulates him at the end. But A. P. Herbert, a friend of Sir Winston and of myself, decided to 'gang his ain gait'. His maiden speech certainly woke the House up and brought forth constant interruptions, some of them acrimonious and heated. The content of the speech does not matter now, but A.P.H.'s unorthodoxy led to a conversation between Winston and him in a corridor outside the Library. They were walking together slowly while Winston explained his feelings and why he doubted whether A.P.H. should have acted as he did, winding up with, 'You call that a "maiden" speech? It was a brazen hussy of a speech.' (Pause) 'It was more: it was a painted harlot of a speech.'

I got to know A. P. Herbert quite well in the House, when he held one of the University seats later abolished by the Socialists. In 1935 we met by chance at Madeira. He was on a cruise in the S.S. *Otranto*, I was in a Royal Mail boat, and a P & O boat was also in harbour at the time. A number of us met at Reid's Hotel.

I found A.P.H. greatly irritated by the dirty habits of the numerous seagulls that surround ships and he wrote a few lines of verse

*Then Chief Whip and now Leader of the Opposition.

which I have never seen in print but which I memorised at the time. This 'Ode to a Seagull' ran:

> O Seagull, we're grieving to see you relieving
> Yourself on the Merchant Marine.
> You have very good sight and should see in this light
> The *Otranto* is not a latrine.
> God gave you the oceans for your little motions
> Or Spain's a convenient po;
> But if it feels finer to aim at a liner
> Well, why not a nice P & O?

I was surprised to be told that *Punch* would not publish this in those days. I can't think why. (Some of A.P.H.'s writings *are* unpublishable but that's another matter.) There is a cheque of his which is in the hands of his bankers, Glyn Mills—or so I have been informed—and the story of it is both harmless and worth recording. He had attended one of the dinners of a dining club to which he belonged but had omitted to pay his subscription. The secretary (whose name was Mumford) reminded him, upon which A.P.H. took a menu card and wrote on the back of it:

> Pay to old Mumford, worst of men,
> The crippling sum of two pounds ten—
> Or to any person white or black
> Whose name is mentioned on the back.

He then drew a little picture of a man, presumably Mr Mumford, and added:

> In case you do not know the chap
> I send herewith a sketch—or map.

By writing in his banker's name and applying a twopenny stamp, which I am sure he had to borrow, the card became legal tender, since you can write a cheque on any piece of paper.

The Churchill-Herbert incident in the House has side-tracked me (one is apt to be diverted by A.P.H.). To return to Churchilliana I remember Clem Attlee at a meeting of Ministers of the war-time National Government, listening expressionlessly while the P.M. discoursed at length on what, in his opinion, should be done. Finally, Winston said, 'Well, gentlemen, I think we can all agree on this course.' Before anyone could say a word Attlee suddenly said, 'Well, you know, P.M., a monologue by you does not necessarily spell agreement.'

This was one up to Attlee, but against this I recall a crack Winston took at him when we were in Opposition. I was passing through the Members' Lobby with Winston one afternoon when some of the Lobby correspondents waylaid him and asked him if he approved of a trip to Australia and other parts of the Commonwealth which the P.M. (Attlee) was then contemplating; it had been argued that the Prime Minister should not absent himself for so long while immediate post-war problems were so pressing at home.

'Ah, I see what you mean,' said Winston. 'While the mouse is away the cats may play?' I lingered behind him and suggested to the Press men that this was not a remark which an ex-P.M. should have made about his successor and asked them not to publish it as it seemed to me somewhat undignified. When I caught up with Winston he asked me what I had been doing. I told him the truth and waited for the reaction with a little trepidation. But he said quite calmly, 'Perhaps you were right.' Actually, the Press did not use it and I was relieved.

Sir Stafford Cripps presented Churchill with something of a problem on his return from Moscow where he had been our Ambassador. This was a Chamberlain appointment, and it came about in a curious way. Cripps came to me in the House one day in late 1939 and said he didn't want to worry the P.M. but would I pass on the message? He wanted Chamberlain to know that he was prepared to serve the Government 'in any capacity' and would, for example, try his hand at managing a factory. Not long after this he was appointed to Moscow, the reasoning being that, apart from his brilliant intelligence, his left-wing Socialist beliefs might make him popular with the Soviet leaders. (I doubt if it had any effect at all. I remember Beaverbrook, after a trip to Russia, telling Churchill that he had taken Cripps along with him to meet Stalin. Cripps had not been invited, and in fact had had no contact with any of the Soviet leaders for six weeks.) However, his experience in Moscow produced in Stafford the idea that he had a message of some kind to deliver on his return and he asked to be allowed to broadcast to the nation. He repeated this request within a few days of his first broadcast.

I was sitting alone in the Smoking Room one day when a well-known Labour M.P. came over and sat down. 'Well, Jimmy,' he said, 'you'll have to watch your step from now on.' I naturally asked him what sort of trouble was being brewed and by whom. He explained that he and a few others were in touch with Stafford Cripps and that they were going to organise an active and vigorous opposition to the all-party National Government.

To say that I was interested is an obvious understatement, but I could not show it. So we talked agreeably for a little and then I consulted my watch and said that I must be going. After a slow exit, I hastened to my room and got on to No. 10 direct. Churchill never failed to function quickly if there was any suggestion of trouble on the way. I told him there was a possible trouble that he should know about and he said, 'Come over now.' I repeated the conversation and he chewed it over for a little. Then I asked if he had seen Stafford yet. 'Yes,' he said, 'last night. I have made him an offer and he is thinking it over.'

Clearly there were two lines of action open to Cripps—office or opposition. I asked the P.M. what he proposed to do now. He replied at once, 'We must enlarge the bait.' The next day Stafford Cripps entered the War Cabinet and, having chosen his course, could not have been a more loyal Minister, little though some of his chores can have suited his restless mind or his political inclinations.

One evening after work and during a refreshment which Stafford would never share, Winston suddenly said to him, 'Stafford, will you take to drinking champagne if I undertake to preach the pure gospel of Socialism?' 'Yes,' said Stafford, 'I agree,' upon which Winston turned to me and said, 'All bets are off.' He then added, 'Isn't it bad luck for poor old Stafford—I drink the champagne and he gets the red nose.'

Stafford had considerable ideas about the manner in which business in Parliament should be reorganised with a view to greater efficiency and acceleration of the machinery of government. He wrote a paper on the subject but it suffered from excessive length; at least it did not attract the man to whom it was addressed and it was passed to me. I read it and commented, pointing out that Churchill himself had advocated some of the ideas in years gone by—e.g. the Finance Bill to be sent to a Committee upstairs to get it away from the floor of the House—and that he must be careful. No more was heard of it and I doubt whether the author got even the formal 'Ack and thank' reply: this was the P.M.'s instructions to his Secretariat when he meant 'Acknowledge and thank', the reply which committed no one to anything further.

In general, he hated committing himself to any course unless and until he had mastered its implication and finally convinced himself that he was on the right lines. If in doubt, his habit was to write 'T. o. B.' at the top of a paper or submission from some Minister. This meant 'Top of the Box' and the paper was put by a secretary in one of the boxes to go to Chequers for the week-end. I said one day to Leslie Rowan, his principal secretary, 'You must have quite a lot of papers at the top of the box.' 'Oh yes,' he answered. 'Several boxes full.'

Most people who were beyond infancy in 1940, or indeed during the following decade or so, must have heard Churchill broadcasting and thereby have retained an impression of his voice. He spoke slowly and impressively, and at times seemed to exaggerate a sort of lisp. He was no mean actor and when dictating any speech he would whisper each sentence quite audibly before dictating it. In this way he got the sound of his words and the rhythm, which was, to him, so important. At the same time he taught himself what he intended to say so that he went on the platform virtually word-perfect.

Almost all speakers suffer from nerves, but he was unusual in that his nerves were worst during composition. As soon as the speech was finished and his notes complete and in order, he reverted to normal and mounted the platform, when the time came, without any sign of nervous anxiety.

I remember meeting him in a waiting room at the Usher Hall in Edinburgh before a big meeting. He asked me if I could fetch him a little brandy, which I did. He then remarked to me that he had been very silly: 'I had finished my speech and should have had a rest. Instead I played bezique at Dalmeny with Eva Rosebery and I'm tired.' Then he went on to the platform and spoke with vast energy for fifty-five minutes—and by then he was well into his seventies.

On another Scottish trip I was alone with him in his bedroom when he was dictating his speech for a big Conservative
meeting that evening, and he was dealing with the subject of private
—or free—enterprise and its merits. He dealt with the objectives
and value of the system upon which British industry had been
built up in the last century, coupled with the fact that there must
be a 'floor' below which no man should sink, but '*no ceiling*'.
In other words, the social services must take care of the disabled
and unemployed, while for the rest the sky should be the limit.
I do not quote verbatim, but he said, in effect, that our aims must
remain 'the profit motive, employment for our people, and service
for the community'.

My role was that of silent audience, but at this point I could
restrain myself no longer and interjected, 'Oh, no. Seriously,
I would alter that.' He turned on me and demanded what my
objection was. I replied that he should not put the profit motive
first. His reaction was immediate and angry: did not I, or the great
Conservative Party, believe in the profit motive? And if not, what
on earth was there for which we *would* stand up? I explained that I
did *not* object to the profit motive but my view was that he should
alter his priorities, putting employment first, service for the
community second, and the profit motive—of which no one need be
ashamed—in third place. He agreed at once and altered his speech
accordingly.

Many of my most interesting and entertaining conversations
with Churchill took place some hours after the curfew had 'tolled
the knell of parting day'. (Incidentally, I have always wondered
why the poet used the word 'curfew', writing in a lonely church-
yard at Stoke Poges. Maybe it scanned better than any other
word and suited his poetic purposes, but the curfew denotes for me
a lock-up or black-out in uncomfortable times. In that case it is
apt enough for war-time nights.) But these talks were by no means
confined to the late-night hours. The interest, amusement, or, at
times, irritation of being with Churchill could be just as operative
at 9.30 a.m. or during Cabinet meetings any time in the day.

One day towards the end of the war, when he was no longer
in any doubt as to its eventual outcome and, as a result, less worried

by military problems, he summoned me to lunch at No. 10. What worried him now were the political clouds, which I also could see, closing in on us, because the better the nation fared in the field of battle, and the more remote any threat of invasion became, the more truculent and difficult did the more tiresome and critical elements in Parliament become—and these were not solely confined to the extreme left or fellow-travellers.

On this occasion he told me we would be alone, as he wanted my advice and wished me to read through some private letters of his own which, he said, were worrying him. I was mystified, but I admit that I was also flattered. I had no idea what to expect as I walked through from my office at No. 12.

He did not drink anything before lunch, but would have a small glass of tomato juice while I got some sherry. As we waited for lunch he produced a bundle of dozens—or hundreds—of 'flimsies' from the past.

I should explain here that even as a young man of no political status he kept copies (or 'flimsies') of every letter he wrote, apart from brief, personal notes to friends. In my time he seldom if ever wrote in his own hand; though he dictated, initialled, and dated everything he issued from his house or office.

He opened this bundle of 'flimsies' at the place he wanted me to start reading and said that he was worried as to whether it would do him any damage as Leader of the Conservative Party if, by chance, the originals of these letters might be sold and see the light of day. He said no more, except to ask me my view, and he then kept silent throughout lunch, whereas I had the dual task of reading and eating. It is never easy to do two things at once but I was aware that my immediate duty was to get on with my reading even if my luncheon, however excellent, had to suffer, as it did.

What interested me first were the dates: the first letter I had to read was dated 1901 and, on turning back for the sake of interest, I found that the file in my hand began with the turn of the century.

Apparently his stockbroker had 'broken' himself at some later date but might still possess the original letters Winston had written to him in the early 1900s. The broker had been a friend, and in the course of certain letters Winston had commented on the possibility of changing his Party—not for the last time! I felt able to reassure him that in my opinion no harm could arise from these letters of long ago. I added that if they should be in danger of coming on the market, steps could be taken to buy them in.

He then told me to see the late Lord Camrose of the *Daily Telegraph*, in whom he had great faith, to confirm my view, which he did.

But in the course of my reading I came upon a letter of 1901 telling his stockbroker to sell some shares to raise enough money to buy a motor-car. I could not refrain from asking him whether he had actually bought a car as early as 1901. (To the best of my knowledge, from about the 1920s he had never been known to drive.) He told me that he did buy the car in 1901. I asked whether he knew how to drive then. Characteristically, he had never thought of being taught but had simply taken delivery and set off. He admitted to 'having a little trouble with a bus'—presumably horse-drawn—near Hyde Park Corner, 'resulting in some damage'. However, he proceeded, 'We got that patched up—*and* in 1902, I myself drove that car all the way from London to York in a day.'

As Winston appeared to have tried almost everything during his early life (and I would commend his book *My Early Life* to anyone seeking first-class entertainment) I asked him whether he had ever played golf, a game to which I have been devoted all my life. After a pause for thought he admitted that he did give it a trial at one time at Walton Heath with Lloyd George. He added, 'You see, he was Prime Minister and I had to keep in touch with him'—a typical explanation.

Churchill was not really a sporting man. He would, for instance, shoot on occasion, if it suited him and he had nothing better to occupy him. Once when he was staying with the Duke of Buccleuch at Langholm, in the Border country, he was one of the guns and the grouse were quite plentiful. He was to address a large open-air Conservative fête the next day. It was at the time when Baldwin's Government was piloting the India Bill through Parliament and Winston was opposing it actively. His mind was obviously concentrated on his speech rather than on the grouse shoot. Shortly afterwards I was shooting over the same ground when my loader, a local forester, suddenly said, 'You should ha'e been in this butt ten days ago.' 'Oh,' I said, 'did you do well?' 'Och,' he replied, 'yon man Churchill was here and I was with him. Ony man could have scored twenty to twenty-five.' The loader was obviously displeased so I asked what Churchill had done. 'Just two,' was the disgusted reply. 'He was walking up and down rehearsing his speech and never tried at all.'

I mentioned this to my host at lunch and he filled in the details. Winston had arrived for dinner the evening before the shoot. In the morning he had appeared at breakfast three-quarters of an hour late, and then only after somebody undertook to do a bit of scouting upstairs and eventually got him down. He then ate one of his normal, very hearty breakfasts. By this time all the beaters, keepers and flankers were miles away and in position but had no signal to start. His host tried to get Winston going, explaining that all the others were already lined up on the distant hill-tops. But all in vain, Winston threw himself into an armchair, ignoring all inducements, and set to digesting the *Scotsman*, with special reference to India.

At long last he condescended to climb into a car and be driven to the scene of action—now about an hour and a half late. After an unproductive morning, he tackled a hearty lunch among the heather. But he was still obviously restless in mind. When he had eaten adequately he asked if he might have a little brandy. His host was not in the habit of carting liqueur brandy on to grouse moors, so Winston announced that he would like a car to take him back to the house to work on his speech for the morrow. I have little doubt that a helpful butler supplied what liquid sustenance was required.

The next day, after newspaper-reading and work on the speech all morning, he did complete justice to luncheon, with accompanying champagne. He was due on the platform at three o'clock but at 2.30 p.m. he was still in the dining-room and his host asked if there was anything he would care to have before embarking upon his enormous task—and a major speech is always that, even for the most skilled and practised speakers. '*Yesh*,' replied Winston, 'I would very much like a bottle of your excellent champagne.' This was brought and I am reliably informed that he consumed two-thirds or more and then mounted the platform, dead on time, and spoke with great force and energy for nearly an hour. Thereafter he ignored most of the guests and local worthies, retired to his bedroom, and slept like a cherubic baby till evening. Which reminds me of once when, while he was shaving, he said to me suddenly,

'Feel my face. Isn't it just like a baby's bottom? But you know that all babies resemble me.'

From time to time, any Prime Minister who holds office for more than a year or so has to change, shuffle or re-make his Government. There are a number of reasons, usually perfectly sound and proper, which necessitate this but it can be an awkward exercise and by no means an easy one, because the Ministers affected may not like it and may not see the point. The sensible and intelligent ones go gracefully because they understand the difficulties of any Head of a Government: others do not because they are ambitious for themselves and resent anything in the nature of a setback in their careers.

Chief Whips are, of course, often consulted on such matters, and there can be sharp differences of opinion, although I have always emphasised that appointments (and dismissals) are the sole responsibility of the Prime Minister.

I once had an argument with Winston Churchill in the garden of No. 10 about a certain appointment he wished to make. I was strongly opposed and said eventually that if he persisted I must resign. On this he became really angry and ordered me out of the place, saying he would expect me at 9.30 a.m. next morning.

When I entered the bedroom in the morning he started at once on a lecture about my position, saying that he only consulted me because he welcomed my advice, but that I had no status in such matters, which rested entirely between himself and the monarch. Since this was a repetition of my own argument, I said at once, 'I understand, Prime Minister, and in view of what you say I withdraw my resignation.' This spoiled his lecture, which might well have gone on for some time. The new man was no good and a nuisance, but the P.M. won and so we settled down again.

On a later occasion a Minister who had been overworking broke down. I could see during a meeting that he was unable to answer intelligently or to concentrate his thoughts: he was in fact on the verge of a nervous breakdown. I had occasion to go to the P.M.'s room just before lunch that day and the position of this Minister—not a member of the Cabinet—was being discussed. This was not my business and I was hastening to get away when the P.M. asked me if I had a suggestion to make as to how to handle the obviously ill man. I replied that he must be relieved at once as I knew he was incapable of carrying on. On being asked how to do this, I undertook to see him off the premises—an offer which was readily accepted.

I found the unfortunate man in his room, looking glassily into space, and explained that in my view he must either go into hospital or go home to bed. His P.P.S. was in full agreement and he telephoned the Minister's wife who quickly got in touch with their doctor and by lunchtime he was away to hospital.

So far so good, but obviously the work, in the House and in the Ministry, had to go on; and yet strangely the P.M. seemed to be at a loss to explain what had happened. I think it was the fear of appearing ruthless or unsympathetic—he never forgot and often quoted what I had told him about the need for a P.M. to be a butcher. But this was simple necessity, not butchery, and we had a gap in our ranks that had to be filled.

I sat down and wrote out a few words to the effect that 'The Minister of X has unfortunately had to be placed on the Sick List. I will make an announcement shortly as to his successor.' I told the P.M. that he could take it from me that the Minister's resignation was, to all intents and purposes, already in his hands, and that I would see to it, so he could do as he wished. The P.M. looked at my brief wording and said, 'I like that. Yes, that's good—*on the Sick List.*'

At the end of Questions that afternoon he rose in his place to make a 'short statement': it went well, because no one is likely to start a discussion about a man who is ill, while the term 'Sick List' covers anything from toothache to bellyache or worse. But this was not the end of the story, because within two or three minutes the Press from the gallery were asking me to let them have the piece of paper from which the P.M. had read, so that they could get the exact words. They had had no foreknowledge of this event and the unexpected statement had taken them by surprise. I said that I would, of course, get it at once and went back to the Front Bench beside the P.M. He was about to pass the paper to me, but he glanced at it first and then said 'No' in a very definite tone of voice. I explained that it was merely for the sake of accuracy. He told me to say that he would let them have it in a few minutes. When he left the Bench he had the statement typed out by a secretary and sent to the Press.

Why? The answer is because it was in my writing and he was not going to let the Press see that while the voice was that of the great man the hand was that of another! All the truly great have their quirks. They accept vast responsibilities but to them also must go the credit. Not that I cared a damn; it was a silly thing, but typical of the way Winston's mind worked.

I had another amusing incident over a Parliamentary question to Winston. Shortly after the Allied victory in the West, Commander Locker-Lampson put down a question to the P.M. asking whether he had any information as to the whereabouts of Himmler. Winston answer was, 'No, sir. I have a great deal of work to do. I expect he will turn up somewhere in this world or the next and will be dealt with by the appropriate local authorities. The latter would be more convenient to His Majesty's Government. I cannot of course speak for our principal Allies.' When I came upon this note I wondered why out of so many thousands of Parliamentary questions which had gone through my hands I had happened to keep this one. Then I realised that it had amused me at the time because the insertion of the word 'local' was in my own handwriting. I suppose I felt that for once I had just slightly improved a Churchillian joke!

↤ XIV ↦

In August 1942 the P.M. flew out to Egypt to visit the Army and then went on to Moscow with the C.I.G.S. (Sir Alan Brooke) and a few others. On his return he invited Attlee, Eden and myself into the Cabinet room, where Brendan Bracken joined us. He talked freely for about an hour and a half. His talks with Stalin, he said, could not have been more frank. He was much encouraged by the firm determination of the Russians to fight on and by their intense hatred of the Germans. Stalin had said this was common to all ranks of his forces and he 'prayed God' they would succeed.

The P.M. was interested by Stalin's repeated references to God. On more than one occasion he had said that he had 'a great respect for God' but regretted that he had 'no divisions to put in the field'. He told the P.M. that earlier, when he was negotiating with the French, he was asked if there was anything he could say or write which would please and help the Pope. Stalin's answer was on the same lines: 'How many divisions has the Pope got?' Churchill told us that in his opinion Stalin was the greatest 'realist' he had ever met. He was also, clearly, a down-to-earth cynic.

Russian production of the weapons of war was on the increase at this time but they wanted us to do more in the West to relieve pressure on themselves. The P.M. was able to explain our own difficulties and intentions in a way which, he said, 'Only personal contact could achieve'. Stalin, he said, had criticised our Navy for leaving behind some merchant ships when a convoy was being heavily attacked. The P.M. explained our methods, and, I think, derived some pleasure from this naval argument, telling Stalin, in so many words, that the Russians had never been a seafaring race and never would understand.

On his last day there his talks continued until the late evening and he was due to leave by plane at 6 a.m. Stalin then asked him if he was 'preoccupied' that night or would he care to come over to his rooms in the Kremlin 'to have drinks'. (The P.M. remarked to us that they don't ask you to look in 'for a drink' but for 'some drinks'. He also said to me alone later, 'As for all this talk about Russian drinking—there is nothing in it. I drank twice as much as they.')

He told me that he and Stalin were alone, apart from an interpreter, in the four-room suite which was Stalin's private quarters in the Kremlin. 'Stalin messed about pulling out a few corks,' Winston recalled. 'Then at intervals a bun-faced woman came in with some odds and ends of food—like radishes.' However, he added that by about midnight 'the table was positively groaning with food'.

Stalin asked Churchill if he would object to Molotov joining them and when the P.M. agreed Stalin himself telephoned. Winston added that Stalin 'seemed to do most things himself'. He was also surprised, he added, that Molotov became 'quite cheerful' and that Stalin 'pulled his leg a good deal'.

My favourite recollection of Molotov is of when he was staying at Chequers and his own detective followed him wherever he went. This bodyguard even re-made his master's bed after the English maid had done it. He made it in such a way that no sheets or blankets were tucked in, so that his poor boss would be able to leap out of bed in a moment in the event of an attempt on his life. Molotov slept with a gun under his pillow while the detective slept, also armed, in the passage. It seemed to me an uncomfortable and trying mode of life.

Stalin told the P.M. that while Molotov was in the U.S.A. he had disappeared once for a whole day; Stalin's view was that he had gone off to Chicago 'to see what tips he could pick up from the gangsters'.

The P.M. also told us that Stalin did not go to bed until about 5 o'clock in the morning because the reports from the Armies did not come in until about four; he started work again about midday.

The P.M. eventually said goodbye to Stalin at 3.30 a.m. and tried to say the same to Molotov too, but Molotov insisted on coming to the airport at 5.30 a.m. to see him off.

I have for obvious reasons not attempted to touch on the matters discussed in Moscow; these are for the military experts and historians. I was fascinated to sit in and hear the P.M.'s vivid description of his experiences, an unusual privilege for a Whip.

One day when we were alone Winston suddenly told me a story he had heard in Moscow—though he did not vouch for its literal truth. There was in Moscow, he had been told, a State-owned night club for officers on leave from the Front. The officers went there with plenty of accumulated pay in their tunic pockets and were able to buy bad champagne, among other things. When they had had a certain number of drinks they were picked up by the Military Police and put in the 'cooler' until they could be sent back to the Front next day. Their pay was confiscated and after paying the bill the balance reverted to the Army Paymaster—or State. Thus the State made a profit on the night club and on the refunded pay which had not been spent, while the Army at the Front benefited by the officers' return to duty long before the expiration of their leave. It struck me that, if the story were true, here at last was a perfect, efficient and profitable case of a nationalised industry!

Pug Ismay (later General Lord Ismay) also gave me a curious example of the mysterious way in which things were organised in this country where all are equal. The British delegation were offered seats for the Bolshoi Ballet and Pug was asked by his opposite number on the Russian staff how many would attend. Six seats were agreed on. But the British party included two warrant officers (N.C.O.s) with four high-ranking staff officers. The tickets were found to be for a good box for four and two seats in the stalls. Pug thought that the sensible thing to do was to use the box for himself and the other generals and to give the stalls to the W.O.'s, who would no doubt be happier on their own and away from the brass-hats.

At the first interval a distressed Russian officer hurried into the box explaining that he had two non-commissioned men in the stalls and that this was not possible because only officers were permitted in the stalls. Pug, always full of tact, apologised profusely, and assured the Russians that he would deal with it. This he did by saying to the couple in the stalls, 'I'm sorry, but you two chaps have to come out—you aren't allowed there so you'll have to come and sit with us in the box. I'll send a couple of generals to fill your seats.'

I have already made it clear that there was no love lost between Lord Beaverbrook and myself in the war years when he was a Minister and we were both very close to Churchill.

It would be an understatement to say that Lord Beaverbrook enjoyed a Better Press than I could command. Not only in his own papers, for I think some of the other Press Lords and proprietors were afraid of him. It is said that 'dog don't eat dog' but if anyone even snapped at his ankles he knew how to bite back, and he also possessed the machinery for retaliatory action. I was interested to be told by a Parliamentary journalist one day that I suffered because I was on 'Lord Beaverbrook's black list' and was to be attacked whenever opportunity offered (or indeed could be manufactured).

I was, therefore, obviously subject to unavoidable criticism, unless I decided to sacrifice myself to this Press Baron. This was impossible; Beaverbrook did not like me, and I regarded him as a political adventurer. There were solid grounds for this mutual antipathy. For one thing, I had been totally opposed to his attitude over the Abdication of King Edward VIII, and I told Winston Churchill later that if he had not been out of office at that time he would have received sound advice and would not have been led astray so easily by men like Max Beaverbrook. Churchill, to his credit, did not dispute this. 'Yes,' he admitted, 'I was doing very well on the sidelines at the time and then this happened. My stock went right down and Baldwin's came up again'—indicating with his hand a rise on Baldwin's side from down near the floor to a height as far above the table as his hand would reach without standing up.

I remarked that I had been in the House when he made his speech and I realised what was about to happen. He was literally shouted down, or almost so. I told him that all 'the boys' (i.e. M.P.s) from the North had been up in their constituencies and had returned after the week-end adamant against the King's marriage. By 'the North' I meant three areas. Lancashire alone returns the same number of Members of Parliament as Scotland, namely

71 each, while Yorkshire returns 52, so the total makes up a formidable proportion of the total in the Commons, whatever line London and the Midlands may decide upon. This is important from a Whip's point of view.

Some time after my troubles as Chief Whip had begun a Ministerial colleague and friend who knew Lord Beaverbrook well and dined with him from time to time said he felt I ought to get to know Beaverbrook better and that he proposed to arrange to take me to dinner with him and 'get us together'. I preferred to turn down this suggestion, saying I would rather sink or swim on my own and be under no obligation to the Beaver. As a matter of fact, I did lunch and dine with him alone more than once later, chiefly at the instigation of Churchill, who, I think, regretted our differences and also wished to patch things up.

One night during the black-out I dined alone with Beaverbrook in his flat in Brook House, Park Lane. After very good and strong cocktails we drank a bottle of excellent hock followed by a bottle of Krug (his favourite champagne) and some brandy. We talked a lot about the war, politics and politicians. Knowing that in the prevailing conditions there was little or no hope of a taxi, I said at about 2 a.m. that I must go, since I had the best part of two miles to walk to my flat in Westminster, and I had to be at Downing Street early in the morning. He asked me if I would like anything before I set off, at which, as is my wont, I suggested that a little whisky and soda would help me on my way.

I had to walk all the way home and was sleeping like a log when to my surprise he rang me at about 8.30 a.m. and asked if I was all right. I assured him that I was and thanked him for dinner, adding that I was grateful to him for a very good sleep, because, on reaching bed, I gave no more thought to bombs or alerts, although I was on the top floor of a nine-storey block of flats. He replied that he had been drunk when I left him and had dropped the telephone when he had tried to ring Fleet Street. I expressed my sympathy and asked what he had done about it. The answer was that he had gone into the bathroom and drunk four glasses of cold water, which he regarded as a first step towards a cure. He added, 'You must have learned to drink in a hard school.'

On another occasion I was sent for by No. 10 Downing Street to go down to Chequers because there was trouble between the

P.M. and Max. I was warned that I was being 'gone for' on the grounds that I had allowed the Labour section of the war-time Government to get away with too much in Parliament—in other words that I was not a sufficiently tough anti-socialist Chief Whip. A car was laid on and I was seen off at about 4 p.m. on a Sunday afternoon by Sir Edward Bridges, then Secretary to the Cabinet, and his assistant Sir Norman Brook, both old friends. I remember them wishing me well and sympathetically hoping that I would enjoy my visit, knowing well that I was feeling ill at the prospect.

However, I concentrated my thoughts on the journey as to how best I could defend myself against these two high-class and loquacious experts in the field of argument and by the time we had reached Shepherd's Bush I had my answer: thereafter I worried no more and went to sleep.

After I had had a drink and a bath we had dinner at the normal late hour. Then there was a long film—as usual; I think it was—not by any means for the first time—*Lady Hamilton*, with its spectacular Trafalgar scenes. The P.M. found pictures dealing with battles irresistibly attractive. I was almost more interested in the energy of Captain Hardy, who landed after the battle beautifully turned-out in an immaculate uniform, and rode off through the night, with his sword clanking beside him, all the way to Norfolk to break the sad tidings to Lady Nelson.

No whisper was permitted during the film and no word of business had been uttered, but at last at about 1 a.m. we adjourned to a quiet sitting-room. There were only the three of us, and it did not long remain quiet. The battle opened and raged: I held my peace, and it pursued its course between the two of them, although aimed indirectly at me. Eventually the P.M. turned to me and asked, 'Have you anything to say?' I said, 'Yes. When it suits you.' He then turned to Max and told him to keep quiet for a minute because 'the Chief Whip had something to say'. When calm prevailed I explained briefly where I stood.

My case was that my instructions, on becoming Chief Whip, were that no controversial legislation was to be introduced unless essential for the successful prosecution of the war. The only exception to this had been the Catering Wages Bill which had been agreed by the Cabinet and forced on me against my will. I added that if my original instructions were to be altered it would be quite simple to engineer the collapse of the National War Government within forty-eight hours.

No more was said.

❧ XV ❧

The Second World War against Germany ended on 8 May 1945 and in July Britain had her first General Election for ten years. The issue as to whether, or when, to bring an end to Churchill's war-time National Government, formed when he succeeded Chamberlain in 1940, was not easily resolved. It was hotly discussed for some time before the decision to go to the country was made.

As always, there was more than one side to the question. With no election since 1935, there were problems which of necessity had remained pigeon-holed far too long. These were matters on which there could be no agreement between the political parties forming the coalition. On the other hand there were those, including myself, who feared that a premature dissolution while the Forces were still abroad and before a Peace Treaty had been negotiated might be regarded as a snap election and do damage to the Conservative cause.

It was easy to argue that the great war leader, Churchill, was an obvious odds-on favourite, and this Beaverbrook never failed to do, pointing to the rest of us as a collection of gutless oafs with perpetual cold feet.

I had a feeling that the Labour leaders, who kept fairly quiet, like myself, were nervous of being blamed for a break-up, and therefore wanted the Prime Minister himself (and the Party behind him) to shoulder the responsibility. As it happened, the faction in favour of the break-up of our not unhappy relationship won, and the result is on record. Churchill, greatly to his surprise, lost the election, and Attlee formed a Labour Government with a large majority.

I suggested to Churchill much later, when an opportunity arose, that while the public applauded him whenever he appeared they voted against him because they were not only sick of war but were afraid of him, because, like Cromwell, he had, in the necessities of war-time leadership, got too much power in his own two hands. For once, he did not argue the point.

But before being kicked out of Downing Street we had an arduous task to perform. Apart from the plans for the election we had in the meantime to remain in office and carry on the task of government. Churchill was still P.M., and he formed what he named the 'Caretaker Government'. The many vacant offices, caused by the departure of the whole team of non-Conservative Ministers, had to be filled; it was not a mere reshuffle but a new Government, containing, of course, all the Conservative Ministers still in office but with the addition of a large number of new ones. It was an interesting though tiresome jigsaw puzzle, which involved me day and night until it was solved. We never let up except to go to bed for four hours or so between 4 a.m. and 8.30 a.m. and we completed the job in two days and nights—or, more precisely, about two and a half eighteen-hour working days.

The P.M. seldom left his bed, eating his meals off a tray beside him. When he wished me to do so I joined him, eating at a small table near the bed. At the end of it all I remember his saying to me, 'Well, that's it and all done by telephone from my bed. Think of poor old Mr Gladstone with all those letters he had to write.' While this was true enough, I couldn't help saying, while laughing also, 'I agree, but *I* haven't seen much of *my* bed.' I got the immediate disarming answer, 'I am so sorry, my dear, I am afraid you have had an awful time. You must get off to bed at once.' Then as an afterthought: 'But you will be back here at half past nine in the morning to tidy up details, won't you?' I told him not to worry.

The following day naturally necessitated several small Ministerial meetings with senior and new Cabinet colleagues. While the telephone did much to help, the task was not at all easy. Some Ministers were out of the country, doing work abroad. I remember that Lord Rosebery, who went to the Scottish Office, was in Scotland, very appropriately, but not in his Edinburgh office, nor at his own house, and in the end the police waylaid him at Cowdenbeath, between Perth and Edinburgh, where he was taken into the police station and put on a line to the P.M.

There were other hitches, of course: some men we wanted could not serve owing to other work, while others in the running were finally decided to be unsuitable. For example, in order to balance things, it was thought that an additional junior post should be offered to one of the 'monstrous regiment...' The P.M. advocated 'Madame X' but for reasons I will not go into here I had to object strongly. He then took up forcefully the case of 'Madame Y'. There seemed to be no really valid objection to her, although I did not like the idea, and she was reached on the telephone. I could hear every word of her high-pitched voice resounding in the bedroom. Eventually I heard her winding up with, 'Thank you so much, darling. That will be wonderful.' This to the man holding the highest office in the land! I felt it wasn't, in the event, going to be 'wonderful' at all, and by this time I was on my feet moving towards the door. The following dialogue ensued:

P.M.: 'Stop! You're not going, are you?'
Me: 'No. I am only going to vomit. I'll be back in a minute.'
P.M.: 'Oh—so you don't like this?'
Me: 'Not much.'

Life is full of interest if one is not bored, and it is often highly entertaining, but it can be tough and at such times it is fatal to weaken, no matter how exhausted one is.

At about eight o'clock in the evening of the 'tidying up' operation I was sitting with the P.M. in his bedroom having a small refreshment when he asked me what I proposed to do. I said that if I got to my club before 8.30 p.m. I could get some food there. He said he would have something in bed, where he was. He then asked what I intended to do afterwards: my answer was the monosyllable, 'bed'. He thought for a moment and then said, 'On your way back, you pass by here, don't you? You might look in about 11 o'clock. That will give us both plenty of time and we could have a little talk.' Once again I gave way, because talk with him was better than bed (or any theatre).

I returned at 11 p.m. and we had talked politics till three in the morning before I asserted myself and said I really must be off to bed, and that he must get some sleep too. So I left him, the formation of the Caretaker Government completed, but not before he had remembered to say to me, 'You'll be back in the morning, of course.'

It was a great relief to have that jigsaw puzzle completed but the resulting Government lived for only about six weeks, when the war-weary public and the battle-weary Servicemen voted against us, though many did not realise that their votes meant that their hero, Churchill, had to go too. This may sound absurd but I am sure it is true; they admired him and meant him no harm. But it was a great blow to Winston.

I suggested to him that he had already done more for his country than anyone could reasonably expect of one man, but it proves how tough he was in body, mind and spirit that he fought on, determined to prove that there was life in the old dog yet. He was seventy-six years old when he fought and won the 1951 election, and he continued in office until he handed over the Premiership at the age of eighty, though remaining in the House of Commons as an ordinary—or rather extraordinary—M.P. He possessed a degree of mental and physical strength, courage, and pertinacy unequalled in this century and probably in others.

It was now our business to organise ourselves as an effective Opposition, but none of us on the Opposition Front Bench had any experience of this, with the exception of our leader, and his claims to fame did not lie in such a role; he had opposed, when out of office, governments of any complexion, but usually playing more or less a lone hand from the sidelines, with no one but himself to organise.

We did our best and the ex-Ministers who had not lost their seats assumed responsibility for the various departments: Anthony Eden, for example, stuck to his Foreign Affairs, while Oliver Stanley took on Finance. We had weekly meetings to discuss the next week's business of the House, of which I was given an advance copy by the Government Chief Whip, Will Whiteley, with whom I had worked closely throughout the war years.

Anthony Eden presided at these meetings or, in his absence, R. A. Butler. Our leader did not often grace us with his presence but remained a law unto himself, taking part in such debates as he wished to. He did, however, always preside over the weekly meetings of the Shadow Cabinet in his own room at the House and he gave a luncheon every fortnight to the entire Shadow Cabinet, plus myself as Opposition Chief Whip.

Effective opposition is not so easy as it may seem. Theoretically, the Opposition opposes the Government of the day but in practice one can't oppose everything. Defence is an example, because it would be foolish—and would look ridiculous —to vote to deny all money required by the three Services. Another difficulty arose over the introduction of the National Health Service. Should it be given an affirmative vote on the Second Reading or should a reasoned amendment be put down? As an original drafter of more than a few motions and reasoned amendments, I know the feeling well. One kicks off cheerfully on paper, inviting the House to welcome a certain Bill and then the fatal word 'but' rears its unavoidable head, and a prolonged period of pencil-chewing and pen-sucking follows.

In the end, there are few alternatives to such phrases as ' . . . but declines to give a Second Reading to a Bill which does not . . . etc'. In effect, this means that the Opposition intends to oppose the Second Reading on certain stated grounds, which sounds reasonable until you read the Government Party's propaganda and the hostile Press which merely state, in so many words, that the Conservative Party is opposed to a Health Service (or whatever it may be).

Any Opposition therefore has to be very careful about what it opposes and how it does so. If a Bill is not opposed flat out on Second Reading it is by no means the end of the story; there still remain the later stages, and many Bills have been mauled in Committee by amendments, whether damaging or constructive. There is also the House of Lords, which provides an admirable revising body, as well as debates which are of a higher order than the Commons.

To me the most depressing and worrying sight of those days was the Government benches in the Commons when we re-assembled after Mr Attlee had formed his Government in July 1945. There sat or sprawled the serried ranks of those chosen by the electorate to represent them for the next five years. They were yelling and shouting with delight and calling across at us in a variety of unparliamentary terms. Worse still, on more than one occasion they resorted to singing 'The Red Flag', while an able and intelligent man like Sir Hartley Shawcross, who should have known better, sank so low as to say in public, 'We are the masters now.' True at the time, perhaps, but this 'mastery' did not survive for more than half the time of Cromwell's tyranny; and after all we politicians are all servants, the elected servants of the public, not masters.

One night some thirty or more Labour back-benchers must have planned in advance a head-on attack on me personally. The business had been of a highly controversial character, and when the division was called at about 10 p.m. and I heard the bells ringing, I left my room to go into the Lobby to vote. I found myself confronted by a barricade of human bodies about five deep blocking the narrow entrance to the Lobby. I pushed and struggled to force an entry but they would not give way and in another two minutes the doors would have been locked and I would have been shut out. I shouted 'Make way!' but they stood with their backs turned to me, well aware of what they were doing.

Then I saw a figure just in front of me, also struggling, and I thought he was in on this game. Actually he had been sent out by Whiteley, the Chief Whip, to render me aid, but unfortunately I did not recognise him in the mob and he was the only man I hit with any force! His name was Taylor, a Labour Whip and a good man. He helped me to get in and I voted. I apologised to Taylor, who understood, and we remained friends.

Perhaps it only goes to show—if further proof were needed—how well-hated Chief Whips are! But it was an outrageous performance and, I believe, quite unprecedented. Official messengers, Lobby correspondents and even police officers, however improperly, came to me privately afterwards, deploring the scene and offering to give evidence on my behalf should I require it.

I never dared tell Winston Churchill of this scene because he was in a bellicose frame of mind against the Government in those days and I did not want him to force me to raise it as a matter of privilege in the House, which I was well entitled to do. My own instinct told me that it was in the interests of Parliament to keep quiet, hoping that thereby our opponents would learn better manners—perhaps from men in their own ranks such as Will Whiteley and James Maxton. I think I was right, even though the Standing Orders of the House, which are read out by the Speaker at the beginning of each new Parliament, lay it down that free access must be guaranteed to all Members so that they may carry out their normal duties.

I was sent for next day by Mr Speaker who informed me that I had every right to raise the matter that day in the House and that he had issued special instructions to the attendants and to the police to ensure that no such behaviour could be repeated. He explained that this had never been done during the hundreds of years of which there were records because no one had ever before acted in such a disgraceful manner.

Next I was visited by Herbert Morrison, Leader of the House, and by the Government Chief Whip (Whiteley), both of whom expressed their apologies and their profound regrets and sympathy. Herbert, with whom I always got on and who was amusing as well as being a good Parliamentarian, assured me that he had given the rebels a real dressing-down that same morning and that I need expect no further trouble apart from normal verbal abuse. Thus without doing anything I enjoyed support and gathered in apologies from all sides: indeed, had I been conceited and had I not been a Chief Whip I might almost have been fool enough to classify myself as popular.

The lesson which I hope and still believe it taught a number of Labour newcomers is that disagreement in politics should not affect personal feelings or friendships. There will always be disagreements and not only between political parties: I have had many disagreements with my own friends but we are all entitled to hold our own views and to express them in or out of Parliament. This should not, however, necessitate the use of physical force in order to impress the other side with the strength of one's own case.

No one can call Parliament as viewed from the Opposition benches an exhilarating sight or experience. The 1945 Parliament dragged on its depressing course month after month and year after year.

I knew the new P.M. to be an excellent Chairman of Committees who never wasted time or uttered an unnecessary word. Presumably, therefore, he was equally efficient in Cabinet. Attlee, unlike Ramsay MacDonald earlier, had the advantage of having at his disposal some ex-Ministers from the war-time National Government who had ability and experience of office. I refer in particular to Ernest Bevin at the Foreign Office, Herbert Morrison leading the House, and Stafford Cripps at the Board of Trade (and later at the Treasury); and no one could say that Aneurin Bevan at the Ministry of Health was a nonentity!

The Labour Government succeeded in introducing more controversial legislation in a shorter space of time than we had thought possible, and another thing we learned in Opposition was the difficulty of working without the expert knowledge of senior civil servants, which is always at the disposal of a Minister in his Department. The top civil servant is not asked to agree or disagree but he can point out the difficulties and advise on the various possible courses. However, we were fortunate in having a good set of younger men in a 'back room', mainly recruited by Rab Butler. Amongst these were Iain Macleod and Reginald Maudling, who worked hard and deserve credit. It was at this time that I first met them and they have risen far since then. These able younger men in our 'back room', where I also had my office, did a lot of excellent briefing for our ex-Ministers in Opposition and for the Party in general and it was Iain Macleod who, after entering the House a little later, was the first man on our side to put a spoke in Nye Bevan's wheel as Minister of Health. Others had tried but failed and it fell to this new, untried outsider (using racing parlance, of course) to breach Bevan's stronghold.

Bevan turned out to be a success as a Minister, and he was also a character and, of course, a first-class debater, often vitriolic but at heart a kind man and good company. While saying that in all sincerity, I still think it was unfortunate that the then Chief of Air Staff, Sir John Slessor, chose to bring Bevan into White's Club on their way home after a late meeting.

I was about to leave for home with Walter Elliot but, being on the committee of the club, asked Walter to wait while I went into the inner room to see if any troublemakers were in evidence. Nye had recently referred in public to the Tories and such people as 'vermin', which had not endeared him to all members of a place like White's. I told the younger members present that he had just been brought in by a member, a distinguished air marshal, and reminded them that he was a guest, as well as a member of the Cabinet, and I advised them to play the hand easy. Then I went off home to bed.

In the morning I read the news that a prominent Minister had been kicked down the steps of White's. (Next day the *Daily Express* published Osbert Lancaster's perfect cartoon of one bishop on the steps of the Athenæum imploring another not to kick a certain pink Dean down *their* steps!) The end of it all was that, knowing Bevan slightly and being on White's committee, it fell to me to convey the club's apologies to him. Strangely enough, it was the unanimous wish of the committee that I should do this job! I did it in person in preference to writing, and Nye Bevan could not have been nicer. He said that it had not been a hard or venomous kick and that it had not actually hurt at all. I told him that we were taking firm action against the offenders, and we did in fact get rid of three members.

Looking back, it is odd to think that I was one of those whose advice Nye Bevan sought, at a difficult moment in his career, as to which line he should take to counter Hugh Gaitskell's bid for leadership of the Labour Party as successor to Clem Attlee. The other obvious contestant was Herbert Morrison, and I, having nothing to lose or gain either way and with no axe to grind nor personal prejudice, was wholly unbiased. Perhaps this accounts for Bevan's purely informal approach to me.

I pointed out to him that he and Gaitskell were the younger of the three starters and that Herbert, being older, had (as an insurance company would say) a shorter expectation of life. Therefore, I argued, his (Bevan's) policy must be to disentrench his troops then opposing Morrison and realign them in support of the elder man in order to defeat Gaitskell. Then, when Herbert would have to hand over to a younger man, he should have a straight fight against Gaitskell, which, by that time, he might win.

He did not contradict me, but remarked upon the difficulty of disentrenching your army suddenly in order to face the other way and support the enemy whom you really wished to defeat. I, in turn, could not deny this, but said that I saw no alternative—upon which we parted amicably.

In addition to our daily work as the Opposition, we had to consider our policy and tactics for the next General Election. Inevitably the time came, before very long, when the question of the leadership became an important problem within the Party.

Winston had passed the 'threescore and ten' mark when we

went into Opposition and there seemed every likelihood that by the time we had a chance to regain power he would be nearer eighty than seventy. Therefore it was natural that by 1947 there were members of the Party, including members of the Shadow Cabinet, who felt that a change of leadership would be better now than later. There was, however, no suggestion that Winston was failing either in mental or physical ability. I say this now because of the very surprising—to me, at least—words of Lord Moran in his book, conveying the impression that Churchill had been going downhill for some time before this.

It was the situation ahead, that of 1950 (or earlier, if anything untoward happened to the Attlee Government), that influenced a number of thoughtful—and in some cases also ambitious—Tories, and at length it was decided that the time had come to take steps to acquaint Winston with the possibly unpalatable news that in the opinion of a body of his colleagues he had 'had it' politically. I was not keen to be involved in the clandestine meeting of ex-Ministers and senior members of the Party which was arranged, but I recognised the force of the argument about Winston's age and I was quite prepared to admit that Leader of the Opposition in peace-time was not his *métier*. As his Chief Whip I felt I ought to attend.

It was not that I thought it would be right for Winston to take on the task of Prime Minister again in his late seventies but —though there are those who will laugh at the idea of a Chief Whip being sentimental—I did want to see this great man find a haven of peace without further political struggle or turmoil, especially within the Party.

I think there were eight of us who finally met to lunch together at Harry Crookshank's house in Pont Street. This was thought to be a discreet place as it was desirable to avoid the attention of the Press. I can think of nowhere better suited to such a purpose. As you entered through the heavily leaded glass door—the glass was of colours calculated to obscure all light—the catacomb-like gloom was relieved only by one small weak electric bulb, like the light on the tabernacle 'dimly burning'. (I was reminded of Hugh Cecil's description of his own house in Bournemouth after his retirement as 'early water closet'.)

We gathered in an upstairs drawing-room decorated with

screens, Eastern *objets d'art*, and uncomfortable Victorian furniture. It was all very serious and intense, and so it continued through lunch. The talk was unrelievedly politics on the highest level; intellectually earnest and in one or two cases highbrow, by which I mean we had among us those deep thinkers whose mental processes will not follow the normal, sensible course of other people, lest that should relegate them to the level of the ordinary and let others forget how clever they are. Such people I find are almost always wrong.

I am not naming any of those present, but I should say that the heir apparent, Anthony Eden, was not among them, on the ground that it would be awkward for him in his position. I did not fail to see his point, which was primarily evasive. There were others not present because of other engagements that day—I was reminded of the biblical parable of the supper guests. However, the exchange of views among those present crystallised into the agreement that, while no one had any thought of inflicting any sort of hurt or harm on Sir Winston, he should be informed that it was probably in the better interests of the Party that he should seek peace in retirement.

It quickly became clear to me that each of my companions had excellent reason for not being the person to convey the tidings to Winston, so I was not surprised that it was agreed unanimously (if you don't count me) that the man for the job was the one who had no axe to grind and was, after all, the Party's Chief Whip!

It was, of course, true that I had no axe to grind, which made me a suitable emissary for what might prove a self-destroying task, recoiling, if it failed, on the political advancement of anybody with what might be called a Prime Minister's baton up his sleeve.

I felt it my duty to convey the considered views of my superior colleagues but I did not welcome the task, and I found its execution both difficult and highly distasteful. I had, however, said to Winston before this that I wondered why, after all he had done already, he did not relinquish the leadership and give himself some rest and a change of scene with more time for painting, so I hoped that he would not be unduly surprised or distressed by my mission. I was wrong.

Winston received me alone in his room at the House. I told him at once that I had a difficult task to perform and that I trusted he would bear with me without being annoyed. He assured me that he would not get annoyed and invited me to proceed. I reiterated my view that no other man had done more than he for his country and then told him of the unanimous view expressed by our colleagues at our meeting. He reacted violently, banging the floor with his stick and implying that I too had joined those who were plotting to displace him.

However, I had done my job, and as he knew I had never been one of Anthony Eden's backers this may have gone some way to soften his feelings against me personally when he cooled down. But it did take a few days before he could treat me normally again. Soon afterwards he informed his constituents that he intended to 'soldier on' until he had turned out the Socialists, which, to his credit and rather to my surprise, he did in 1951 after the near-miss of 1950. No more was heard of his retirement for several years and none of the others present at our private meeting repeated to him the views which they had so kindly invited me to convey.

In 1947 I was unwell and had to undergo an operation to my antrum due to poison collecting under my left eye. I went off to Arizona to recuperate, thanks to the generosity and hospitality of my friends, Herbert Agar and his wife, Barbie.

Thus I eventually got Winston Churchill to accept my resignation as his Chief Whip. I was relieved by Patrick Buchan-Hepburn and joined Winston's Shadow Cabinet instead.

I might add here that persuading Churchill to accept my resignation as his Whip was no easy business. It was not that he had anything against my successor, whom he knew well, but that he disliked change of any sort. I had explained to him more than once that it was time for me to go. Then I told him one day that I was about to go into hospital and I would like him to accept my resignation because it was not fair to my successor that he should do the work while I nominally held the job (unpaid though it was).

After a little thought he said he had to go to his dentist somewhere around Harley Street and that I could explain it all to him in his car on the way. This was, of course, merely a device by which to get a companion for the journey rather than travel alone, which bored him. In the car he agreed that I should write him 'a little letter—not more than one page, dear'—of resignation. We then discussed how I should begin my 'little letter'. I said that to address a man in his position as 'Dear Winston' sounded to me too familiar if not cheeky: so we settled on 'Dear Mr Churchill' and we parted at the dentist's door.

I was driven back to the House and wrote my 'little letter' which I delivered personally into his hands before going into hospital. With my own eyes I saw him put the letter into his pocket. Soon after coming out of hospital I left for Arizona, but nothing happened. Then I wrote to David Margesson asking him to prod the Great Man's memory and get him to act. But still nothing happened and I returned in due course from America. I then saw this extraordinary man again in person and asked him why he had not yet published my letter of resignation. He looked at me with a very disarming sort of half-smile and said almost apologetically, but like a naughty little boy, 'I suppose I must have lo*sh*t it.' So I wrote another 'little letter', which he did answer and publish.

❧ XVI ❧

The period which followed my resignation as Chief Whip in 1947 provides an interlude in which I would like to set down some personal and not at all profound reflections on life in politics, and to touch on some relationships, without which my story would be incomplete.

One of the first essentials in running the machine of British government is that the opposing forces should understand each others' viewpoint and be sensible enough to organise business by talks behind the scenes; and by this I mean nothing wrong or underhand. Winston Churchill was once kind enough to say that I knew 'how to manage people'. That was the essence of my job. When I left the office of Chief Whip in Opposition, Herbert Morrison generously remarked to me, 'I wish you'd come back, Jim, and help to keep that old man of yours in order.'

That recalls to my mind a serious row which broke out between Winston and Morrison at the time of the change of government in 1945. Morrison had criticised 'unconditional surrender' in a public speech, implying that it had caused unnecessary suffering by bombing—for example in his own London constituency. 'Unconditional surrender' was the policy agreed by the British Government and America, and Herbert, as a member of the Cabinet, had no right to criticise a Government decision. Winston was furious, quite rightly, and said so in public as well as in private.

On top of that, he ordered me, as his Chief Whip, to have no dealings with Herbert, who was then acting as Leader of the House for Attlee, the new P.M. Winston was quite violent about this and I was disturbed, but eventually, when he paused for breath, I ventured to explain that he was placing me in a serious difficulty, because I had to see Morrison, along with the Government Chief Whip, two or three times a week to arrange the business for the following week. (I might add that my own great leader was not especially interested in our business unless it affected himself, but left it to me and the Leader of the House, with his Chief Whip, to arrange things.)

Winston looked at me, chewing his cigar and sipping at his glass. I could almost hear him thinking. He had taken my point, which was, in effect, that the machine had to be kept turning. He was rehearsing his words to himself, under his breath, as he did when dictating his speeches to his 'young ladies' of the secretariat. Eventually the Oracle made a characteristic utterance.

'Yes,' he said, 'I see your point. But while the firing will continue between the opposing forces this does not mean that messengers may not pass between the lines.' I thanked him and that was that. Another seeming crisis was amicably averted.

I am sure many people outside Parliament do not realise how often good *personal* feelings exist between M.P.s of all types and shades of opinion; how many genuine friendships, based on mutual respect and human liking, are formed irrespective of party affiliations. I can see Winston Churchill seated in the Smoking Room with a Trade Union leader, with whom he was on the friendliest of terms, and conducting a heated but entertaining argument over his shoulder with Aneurin Bevan at an adjacent table—both enjoying themselves to the full while the Members around, of any party, listened and laughed.

Good men of all parties know that the first need is that the wheels of government must continue to turn, and to that end differences of opinion are sunk and good relations maintained. When my old friend David Margesson died in 1965 Lord Attlee wrote a brief tribute in *The Times*, of which this—by a Socialist leader of a Tory Chief Whip—is the final sentence: 'I always recall with gratitude his unfailing courtesy and consideration to our small band, whose difficult task he recognised.' He was referring to the situation after the overwhelming Socialist defeat in 1931. But people like Attlee, Herbert Morrison, Ernest Bevin and others all understood as well as we did the necessity of keeping the machine running smoothly at best or, at worst, grinding over the hard places.

An example of genuine personal friendship achieved naturally despite unalterable and total differences politically was that between James Maxton and myself. Maxton was the M.P. for the Bridgeton division of Glasgow and leader of the Independent Labour Party in Parliament. He spent six months in prison in the First World War for his anti-war and pacifist attitude and speeches. I once asked him if he had any bitterness about his time in prison. 'Not at all,' he said at once. 'It was the best rest I ever had in my life.' The Governor had allowed him an ample supply of books and he had caught up with quite a lot of reading.

Maxton was a truly beautiful speaker who could, at will, reduce the House to silence or tears, rouse it to anger—or laughter. He never used a note, but he possessed the gift of true oratory.

After Maxton's speech following the death of Mr Speaker FitzRoy, Winston Churchill turned to me on the Front Bench and said, 'I wish I could do that.' He then walked across to the bench below the gangway opposite to congratulate him.

Maxton would very seldom enter the houses of his opponents: certain people were apt to lionise him and he hated it. He did enter mine one day when he happened to drop me off at my very small house in Buckingham Place, Westminster. He stopped opposite and looked at the outside of the house and then he asked me if that was the best I could do. 'Where are the flunkeys?' he asked. I urged him to come in as it was my eldest son's seventh birthday and there would be some children and a handful of friends. He came in and became at once the life and soul of the party, although he simply sat quietly drinking endless cups of tea. But he charmed all who could get near him.

He would never touch strong drink but he could smoke cigarettes and drink tea until the cows would have tired of waiting to come home. He often confided to me his latest and best stories, which were also unprintable. I remember him once signalling me from across the gangway to come over to him. As I sat down beside him, he said, 'I can't come over to you and sit on the Government Front Bench, but look as though we are discussing business and don't laugh. I'm going to tell you my latest story.' When he had finished, and I had with difficulty kept a straight face, I asked him if he had told this to his colleague and close friend, the Reverend Campbell Stephen, another Clydeside M.P. 'Oh, no,' he said seriously, 'dinna tell Campbell. He wouldna like it.' I asked why it should be inflicted on me, to which the reply was, at least by implication, that I was unshockable.

The Clerk of the House, Sir Gilbert Campion, said to me one day when, as Chief Whip, I was discussing future Government business with him, 'You are lucky that Maxton was born idle.' I asked what he meant and he replied, 'If he had *not* been born idle he could have done anything.'

James and I spent more than a little of our time talking together on many subjects, not confined to politics. He also shared my love of golf!

One example of his thoughtfulness for others, although totally opposed in politics, was when my friend and secretary, Charles Harris, told me one day in the office at No. 12 Downing Street that Mr Maxton wished to see me when convenient. I was very worried at the time by Party troubles and by the P.M., who was bullying me, but I had no knowledge that Maxton was aware of this, and there was no reason why he should have been.

When he arrived Charles Harris showed him in and I asked him what the trouble was. From his armchair, with his long black hair flowing carelessly about his fine head, he explained in his beautiful voice that he had asked Charles Harris to tell him when I would not be too busy so that he could look in without interrupting me. Then he said, 'Well, James, you know I haven't come to cause you trouble. I ken fine you've had plenty to worry you but I wanted to see you when you had a few free minutes because I've got a new story I thought you would enjoy.' And he proceeded to tell the story, as usual in doubtful taste and un-printable.

But this meeting had been organised quite deliberately by a pacifist left-wing Socialist, via a civil servant, to give a Tory Chief Whip what the Scots would call a 'wee relax' in the worst days of war! It was a kind and thoughtful gesture and I deeply appreciated it.

I possess one or two charming letters from him, written when he was dying of cancer (and knew it). The last bears the address of the Royal Cottage, Stronachlachar, lent to him, I believe, by the Glasgow Corporation who own the land, surrounding the sources of Glasgow's water supply. He wrote:

'My dear James, you will be surprised to hear from me from

an address like this, where Queen Victoria opened the Water Works (I mean the Glasgow ones) in 1890-something.'

Another of the original fire-brand Clydesiders was David Kirkwood. A retired Glasgow police sergeant told me years later that in the days of the 1918 riots he had got David Kirkwood down in the gutter and could easily have broken his neck. He asked whether I thought he had done right to refrain! I replied gravely that he had certainly done right and should not worry any longer because, at the end of it all, David was a good patriot and citizen, and was doing no harm. He even finished up in the House of Lords!

Geordie Buchanan, the member for the Gorbals division of Glasgow, asked me one night in the Smoking Room, when we were sitting late, how as Chief Whip I managed with my home life. How did my wife put up with it? I told him that my wife went to bed, and to sleep, about 10.30 p.m. or so, whatever happened. He eyed me with a degree of dubiety and said, 'Ye mean that? My God, Jimmy, ye're bloody lucky. I've seen me coming up the stairs at one o'clock in the morning fair frightened for ma life.'

Once, when discussing the overcrowding and slums of Glasgow and the question of rehousing, he added, 'But I dinna want any garden in the open spaces for myself. They'd only make me work in it.'

All the 'Red Clydeside' rebels of the I.L.P. of 1918 toned down with age: the major influence on them was James Maxton, who believed that there was nothing to be gained by being rude to one's opponents and never indulged in venomous personal attacks or bad manners.

John Wheatley, whom I did not know personally, was probably the ablest politician of this group, but he could be vitriolic. He died early, after being Ramsay MacDonald's Minister of Health in the first Labour Government. He recognised how vital the slum problem of Glasgow was, and worked hard in and out of office to alleviate it.

The truth is that Glasgow grew up suddenly into a great city and men had to be housed near to their work—mainly the shipbuilding yards of the Clyde. If you look at those three- or four-storey tenement buildings you will see that the stonework outside is solid. But inside, with the common stair and the flats (often single-roomed) leading off, no modern sanitary arrangements were provided. The tenants had to walk down two or more flights of stairs to reach a place which sometimes did not even enjoy a flush of water. This deplorable state of affairs was not due to greedy landlords or to bad building; it was the normal way for those days. But the conditions became terrible with the passage of time and although great efforts have been and are being made to rebuild and rehouse the people, there are those who still suffer. In these areas, such as Gorbals, for example, anti-landlordism and Socialism found a perfect breeding ground.

With Wheatley gone, the leadership of the Clydesiders fell to James Maxton, supported strenuously by George Buchanan, Campbell Stephen, and one or two more. While in London, four of them shared a lodging and I asked Jimmy once how they managed or 'made do', and who did what? He said it worked out all right and explained that one of them did the housework and another cooked, made tea, and so on. I asked what part he played. He replied that someone had to think and plan—do the mental labour —and that he stayed in bed, drank tea, and directed operations. There must always, he added, be a controlling brain on any job.

I made a lot of friends in the House but they all belonged to the Tory or Labour Party. I do not think that I have ever suffered or enjoyed the friendship of a Liberal. I regard this as fortunate for they form a race apart, sitting on the fence and incapable of deciding whether to jump down on one side or the other. It must be a great worry to them and I thank God that I was not constructed that way, even though I may be less intelligent than, say, Lady Violet Bonham-Carter.

Her father (Asquith) was also a highly intelligent, sensible man who was a good Minister and Prime Minister until the First World War undermined him through the machinations of Lloyd George and Max Aitken (Lord Beaverbrook), using Bonar Law as a Conservative mouthpiece. Thus Asquith was brought down and Max Aitken, not for the first time, triumphed—and thus, also, was the once great Liberal Party ruptured so badly that it has never recovered, and appears to me today to be incapable of recovery.

The country in general looks to one of the two great parties to rule and the other to complete our form of parliamentary democracy in Opposition. There appears to be no place for a third party, but I will always regard 'Independents' as welcome additions if they can get themselves elected.

The great Gladstone changed his Party and reached the summit for, in the opinion of many of his colleagues, too long. It is perhaps a pity that he ever changed; he would have made a good Tory. Winston Churchill, on the other hand, saw the light and rejoined the Tories from the Liberals, but when discussing this subject he always took the trouble to explain that it was not that he had altered his political views, but that the Conservative Party had moved to meet him! He was not, in truth, a Conservative at heart, but I will leave to others to decide as to the factors which led to his conversion. He was a law unto himself.

Ernest Bevin, Minister of Labour in the war and Foreign Secretary in the Attlee Government of 1945, was a fine man and a loyal colleague. He was also very good company and would enjoy sitting in the Smoking Room of the House of Commons swopping stories. He could also digest quite a lot of whisky without apparent effect. I was asked once by a friend of mine how much whisky an average whisky drinker could consume without noticeable damage in the course of a sitting. After some thought, I replied, in my view, two-thirds of a bottle but that this would be a lot. My friend said he had asked me because he was not a whisky drinker but he had watched the Foreign Secretary consume not less than a bottle and a quarter at a party between 6.30 and 7.45 p.m. However, he did not drive a car and anyhow there were no 'breathalysers' then.

When Mr Attlee formed his Government after the Labour Party's sweeping victory in 1945, Ernie Bevin was originally destined for the Treasury, and told me this. However, he was switched to the F.O. before any announcements had been made public, while Hugh Dalton was sent to the Treasury. There was so much anxiety and distress caused by the thought of Dalton at the F.O. that Attlee was forced to change his mind.

I was in the Members' Lobby one afternoon when Bevin and Dalton were arguing about appointments and plans. Hugh Dalton never suffered from any excess of discretion and was annoyed over the new dispositions. Ernie Bevin knew that I knew what had happened, although I was of the Opposition and, strictly, should not have known. In the end, winking at me behind Hugh's back, he remarked, 'Well, I don't see what you've got to grouse about. I thought I was going to have a nice quiet time at the Treasury and now you've got it.'

I remember meeting Bevin coming out of the Smoking Room one day, his great flanks heaving with laughter. I said it must have been a good story and I was sorry to have missed it. 'Yes, Jim,' he answered. 'You would have enjoyed that.' And he pointed to a corner of the room where a prominent left-wing Socialist was sitting—a man he did not like. He said, 'You see that silly —— over there? Well, he's just been telling me that his wife's age group is next for the call-up, and what should he do about it. I told him there was only one thing he could do and that was to get his wife in the family way, and that my Ministry wouldn't even ask who the father was!' The couple in question were childless.

I asked him once when he was Foreign Secretary and had just returned from some conference in Paris whether he had had a good time. 'Oh, well,' he said, 'you know what it is—all talk, talk. But it was a lovely place, that Palais Rose, and there were lots of lovely NYMPS (*sic*), and you would have loved them, Jim, but you couldn't get at them: they were all up on the ceiling.' I commiserated, adding that I hoped nevertheless he had been able to enjoy himself, to which his answer was—'Well, I had lots of nice little sleeps during the talk but, you see, the old lady came with me too to look after me and taking your wife to Paris is like taking an 'am sandwich to a picnic.'

I was asked by the King's principal secretary one day during the war what the consequences would or should be politically if anything should happen to the P.M. (Churchill). I said that, of course, Anthony Eden was the P.M.'s second string Conservative— and we were the biggest Party in the National Government. I touched also on Attlee's position as Leader of the second great Party but I added, 'You should not, however, ignore Ernest Bevin. He is the most forceful character in the Government apart from the P.M., and he has a large following in the country among the whole Trade Union organisation.'

This, I think, surprised the private secretary, who was a close friend of Eden and had more or less taken for granted that I would back Eden without doubt or question, especially in view of my position as Conservative Chief Whip.

Bevin liked Lord Beaverbrook no more than I did, and this leads me to an extremely awkward situation which developed in about 1943 involving both of them and Eden, as well as the P.M.

Beaverbrook conceived the astonishing idea that our national interests, in those days of trouble and strife, might be in better hands than those of our truly great war leader, Churchill. His plan was to form a triumvirate consisting of Eden, Bevin and himself! Mad as it may seem—in addition to being bad—this scheme was confided to the other two. Bevin's immediate reaction was to take the earliest opportunity of telling the Prime Minister. He said that the P.M. wouldn't believe it of his old friend, but there it was; it was no good suggesting that Bevin was a liar, because he must have realised that evidence could be provided. As to what happened in secret session between the two old friends, I have no knowledge; nor have I as to Anthony Eden's reactions, but it is possible that he may have been flattered and enjoyed the idea of rising higher in the political world. The period of labour was short and the ill-conceived infant was, thanks to Ernest Bevin's loyalty, stillborn.

A close friend of Bevin, to whom he confided this amazing piece of history, asked how it was that the P.M. could retain as a close friend any man who had behaved in this way. Ernie Bevin's reply was, in effect, 'Well, you see, it's like this: it's as if the old man had married an 'ore. He knows what she is, but he loves her.'

The Press plays an important but far from irreproachable part in politics. I have no intention of being such a fool as to criticise the Press as purveyors of *news*: this was their origin, and serious factual news benefits all; it is when they are not being *news*papers that the trouble is apt to come. And the trouble today, in my opinion, is that the political columnists all too often write without knowing all the inside facts of the case. Worse still, in the less responsible papers they often write highly critical paragraphs about Ministers and others carrying heavy responsibilities simply (or so it seems to me) when they cannot think of anything else to write.

The 'popular' Sunday papers are the worst; for example, the Beaverbrook theory seems to have been that the way to attract attention is to attack—whether or not the man attacked really deserved censure. I suppose that this line sells better, and of course to applaud a Government or a Minister is to risk being thought a yes-man.

All I would ask of such journals is to be fair, regardless of the Party to which any Minister may belong. I regard the existing method as dirty, having suffered myself and seen many others suffer too. I would like to see adopted more widely the Christian maxim 'Do unto others . . .'.

I have always tended—wrongly or unwisely perhaps—to keep the Press at arm's length if possible, an attitude based on the good old maxim about using a long spoon when supping with certain people. (I mean 'the Press' in general, for I have many personal friends in the newspaper world—both journalists and proprietors.) The *Express* newspapers, and in particular the *Sunday Express*, never failed to go for me on the slightest pretext and I often wished I could see one of these clever-clever columnists in charge of a big Government department and answering awkward questions in Parliament. The public who trouble to read these political gossips may get the impression that it is easy to give the quick, sensible, or clever answer and that the politician who fails to do so is either a fool or a knave or both. But what one said can in fact be presented unfairly—or out of context—or twisted, accidentally or otherwise.

So much of what they do is simply being wise after the event— the easiest thing in the world. I shall be able to tell you whether sanctions worked or not *after* the Rhodesian mess has dragged on to its sorry end. But I won't say 'I told you so' if I didn't tell you so. The sort of Press I am talking about nearly got Stanley Baldwin down in 1924. Why, I wonder? Orders from their Press Lords, exercising 'power without responsibility'? Baldwin was about to quit, but he was persuaded to stay by the good, sensible, and loyal Willie Bridgeman (Home Secretary) and one or two others, perhaps, against the views of our own Conservative Central Office of the day. I am glad to remember that he then continued as Leader for a further twelve full years.

Churchill seemed to escape the Press fire, but then they were frightened of him as a popular war hero, and of course he had an ally in Beaverbrook. They got down our best man of his time— and a popular Leader—Sir Alec Douglas-Home, who had sacrificed himself in the national interest. Why, I ask again? Some ass or asses said he didn't photograph or televise well! And a lot of silly young back-bench M.P.s followed this absurd line. I wonder how Disraeli, Gladstone or Salisbury (the P.M.) would have fared and what difference their pretty or ugly pictures would have made to their ability to perform their onerous duties.

☙ XVII ❧

When Mr Attlee appealed to the country in February 1950, as he was bound to do in the normal course, having been in office since 1945, the Labour majority was reduced to eight, and while able to hold on for a time they could only do so with difficulty, and controversial legislation had to be set aside. The rash and stupid dictum 'We are the masters now' had, in fact, held good for only five years, for the Conservative Opposition was now in a position to be really effective and to worry the Government incessantly with late sittings.

Hugh Gaitskell, who succeeded Stafford Cripps at the Treasury, upset his own Party by imposing a charge on National Health Service prescriptions, thus causing the resignation of two of his principal colleagues, Aneurin Bevan and Harold Wilson, who regarded this as a breach of principle. Then Ernest Bevin, the Foreign Secretary, and Cripps both fell ill.

Parliament was dissolved in September 1951 and in the election which followed we were returned with a small majority (sixteen) just enough to enable Churchill to form a Government, which he had no hesitation in doing at the age of seventy-six.

The declaration of the poll in Elgin, headquarters of my constituency, did not take place until the early afternoon. Having returned thanks to those assembled in the street there, I had to go on to repeat this in the High Streets of Forres and Nairn. Then I had to travel south, which meant a considerable delay compared with those candidates—including Sir Winston—whose polling results were announced before or after midnight on polling day.

My home in Moray is about 570 miles north of London but Winston could never understand why I could not get back to London as soon as he. I learned afterwards that he had given instructions to the police and the A.A. patrols all the way south to intercept me and tell me to go straight to him at Chartwell, where he was forming his new Government.

They did not catch me, probably because my brother and I turned off the Great North Road to avoid traffic. I was exhausted after electioneering and my brother kindly drove my car a large part of the way. On reaching London, after doing the lap from Edinburgh in a day, I had a message from an old friend, Harry Crookshank, who then became Leader of the House and Lord Privy Seal, that I was to be at Chartwell at midday next day and that he would pick me up in the morning and drive me down.

When we arrived I was amused that Winston took full credit for having been so clever as to put the police on my track and intercept me on the way south. I did not argue the point or explain that I had merely come as quickly as I reasonably could and with no knowledge of his intentions as to my future. But in fact all that had been in my mind on the way down from Scotland was that, the result of the election being what it was, I ought to get in touch soon in case he should have any use for me or my advice as his past Chief Whip and member of his Shadow Cabinet. However, on the journey from London to Chartwell Harry Crookshank had forewarned me as to what lay ahead and I was ready with my thanks for the compliment and my regrets that I was unsuitable for what he proposed.

Immediately we arrived the P.M. took me into a sitting-room alone and said, 'I want you to go to the Scottish Office.' I said my piece as planned, but he persisted. I, in turn, insisted that I knew little or nothing of the varied responsibilities of that office. He asked me what other post I had in mind as being agreeable to me. I told him 'None,' but assured him that I would, of course, support him and his Government in Parliament. I added that in office I would only let him down. He took my arm and said, 'No, you won't.' I have often said that his powers of persuasion were remarkable. Anyway, before luncheon I found that I was a Secretary of State and in the Cabinet.

To be strictly truthful, the Scottish Office had never been one of my ambitions. Politically, my ultimate ambition was achieved when I became Chief Whip, but this does not mean that

I have any regrets about my time as Secretary of State for Scotland. It was simply an unexpected honour, and I am proud to have been given the opportunity to serve Scotland to the best of my ability.

It is said that Lord Melbourne was reluctant when first approached to become Leader of his Party and thereafter Queen Victoria's first Prime Minister. A sensible friend persuaded him by suggesting that, even if he felt reluctant, it would be 'a very good thing to have done' and satisfactory to look back upon. Without bracketing myself with men who have reached such heights, I suppose that my feelings about the Scottish Office and a seat in the Cabinet bear some similarity to the feelings of Lord Melbourne on his loftier plane.

But to return to that day at Chartwell, once the matter of my personal future was disposed of Winston produced a half-sheet of paper with a few names on it, presumably supplied by the Chief Whip, representing those M.P.s and peers thought suitable for me to have as my Minister of State (a new office) and Under-Secretaries. I did not like the look of parts of this document and said so. The P.M. was, naturally, very busy and had to get on to other problems but before leaving me he said, 'All right, you get hold of one of my young ladies and get her to write down what you want.'

I did so, and in the first place asked for Lord Home as my Minister of State. I got this, and everything else I asked for. I had not sought the job and the P.M. knew this, as he also knew that I genuinely doubted my own ability to see it through, but never from that day until the end did he fail to give me his help and his support, often fighting my Ministerial battles for me.

I was certainly right in my choice of Alec Douglas-Home, as the P.M. also knew and probably realised even more fully when two or three years later both Lord Salisbury and Anthony Eden wanted him to leave me in order to strengthen their offices. The P.M. told me himself of these requests for Alec's services, adding, 'Your Home, Sweet Home seems to be doing well.'

But to return to 1951, the old warrior moved his chattels back into No. 10 Downing Street with no sign of doubt or anxiety as to his ability to govern on the score of age or any other. He did not possess what are called 'nerves'; he was made for responsibility.

This was the time when the need for rebuilding Downing Street was said by the experts at the Ministry of Works to have become urgent, as it was subsiding; apparently the foundations were already two feet ahead of the bottom of the house, which was resting insecurely on mud. The resuscitated Prime Minister would have none of this. As he remarked to me one day, 'After all, if it did fall down, one would probably have gone out to tea.' Since he never went out to tea nor drank it in the afternoon this struck me as unlikely.

The new Government, with its slender majority, had to settle down and get into harness. The Party was, of course, in good spirits, elated by our moderate success which had at least dislodged the Socialists after six years, but many controls and even war-time rationing were still operative, and good spirits do not last long unless results are visible.

As Lord Woolton put it in his memoirs, 'We had also a heavy load of promises.' These included the abolition of controls, or 'setting the people free', and legislation to repeal Socialist acts imposing nationalisation in certain cases.

A well-remembered example of our difficulties was the Crichel Down case, which dislodged my old friend Tommy Dugdale (Lord Crathorne) as the Minister responsible. It was bad luck and no direct fault of his own. On the credit side of the balance sheet, Harold Macmillan scored a significant success at the Ministry of Housing, assisted by Ernest Marples as his Under-Secretary in the Commons, and Lord Mills. This success probably had a considerable effect on feeling in the country because housing was one of the outstanding problems, thanks to the absence of war-time building and, of course, destruction by enemy bombing. It is also a subject which is purely domestic and easily understood, being close to the hearts of all.

We had promised to work up to a total of 300,000 houses in a year, whereas the Socialists had stuck at 200,000 and said that we could do no more. Our target was achieved and even a little exceeded in three years. I was close to this in the Scottish Office as we had to do our utmost to keep pace, houses being needed no less in Scotland. Harold Macmillan always kept in close touch with our Scottish experts, and helped us all he could, and I would pay special tribute to Tom Galbraith (now Lord

Strathclyde), my Under-Secretary, whom I asked to apply himself particularly to this vitally important matter. Indeed it had been he who moved and carried the resolution naming 300,000 as our target at the Conservative Party Conference preceding the 1951 election.

Harold Macmillan, by his success and the proof of his administrative abilities at Housing, greatly enhanced his political stature and his place in public esteem; had he failed, his popularity at a very important later date might not have been sufficient to get him the door-key of No. 10 Downing Street.

It is not, however, my intention to rehearse here a list of the Government's successes or trials or errors; any student may find this in the official records of the period.

An unexpected and sad blow fell on the nation in February 1952. King George VI died. He had been ill, but it was thought that he had recovered to a great extent, although never a strong man physically. In addition to the general feeling of loss, my personal sympathies went out to the new Queen. She was so young, and I could not help feeling that it would have been less of a strain for her to undertake such a task ten or even five years later.

I attended the Privy Council meeting dealing with Her Majesty's formal accession to the throne and I was privileged, as Secretary of State, to be one of those who signed on behalf of Scotland. It was an impressive and melancholy ceremony.

Afterwards I walked out into the Mall in my Privy Councillor's uniform to find my car when I was signalled by George Buchanan, the Glasgow left-wing ex-M.P. who had left the Commons to become Chairman of the Public Assistance Board after being an Under-Secretary at the Scottish Office in Attlee's Government. I had not seen him for a year or so and having always liked him I went over to ask how he was faring. He ignored my greeting and said, 'I never thought ye were such a bloody fool, Jimmy.' 'I'm sorry, Geordie,' I said, 'but what have I done wrong?' 'Och,' he said, 'to take on that job at the Scottish Office. Ye'll never make a bloody thing out o' that.'

We never met again before his death. Then I recalled vividly his taking leave of some of us in the Smoking Room at the House after his long years as an M.P. Walter Elliot, who was beside me, said, 'You'll miss this place, Geordie.' 'No, I won't,' he said. 'I've lost the power of hating.'

XVIII

Prime Ministers normally do not have the time to get around to browbeating or pestering their Ministerial heads of departments. So long as a Minister keeps out of trouble and runs his department smoothly, without anything worse than the normal attacks and smear campaigns from his opponents in Parliament, he may be left in comparative peace, and I was fortunate in this respect. When the P.M. sent for me, outside of normal Cabinet meetings, it was to ask my views on some matter unconnected with my office.

But I have to confess that while I was Secretary of State for Scotland I did suffer a defeat. It was while I was piloting a Bill affecting St Andrews University, and I had been warned that I was likely to be defeated in the Scottish Standing Committee if I did not give way. But I believed that I was right and I had given instructions that the Bill should be drafted uncompromisingly on my lines, fortified by the knowledge that I was following the advice of two expert inquiries, the report of one of which had been written by a most capable lawyer, Lord Cooper, late Lord President of the Court of Session. The details are of no consequence now; the point is that I was defeated, and in the House this always leads to shouts of 'Resign'. I was then asked seriously by whoever was leading the Opposition in Committee as to my intentions. I replied that I intended to proceed with the rest of the Bill—which I did.

At the end of that sitting, Sir Charles Cunningham, the distinguished civil servant then head of the Scottish Home Department, who was well aware of the danger throughout the proceedings, asked me what I wished to do. I decided to go ahead but not to try to reverse the Scottish decision at the Report stage, which would later come before the whole House in Committee. I did not like the idea of a Scottish decision upstairs being overturned by English votes later—and anyhow it was not the end of the world, politically or personally.

But I also told him that I must report to the P.M. and I asked him to arrange an appointment for me at No. 10. I must say for the P.M. that he always saw me at once when I did ask because, I think, he knew that I would never bother him unless I had to, but I have a feeling that Cunningham was a little worried about this particular request of mine. To satisfy him as to the importance of the occasion I explained that I must offer my resignation.

It worked: I was told to go straight over to No. 10 and I was shown directly into the Cabinet Room where Winston was working on his papers. Without troubling to look up, he asked what I wanted. I told him of my defeat and, still not looking up, he asked what I intended to do. I replied, 'Proceed with the Bill.'

'All right,' he said, 'is that all?'

I explained that a defeat on a Government Bill was a serious matter and that I felt it my duty to place my resignation in his hands. At this he did look up and said with some irritation, 'I do wish you would stop talking nonsense and leave me alone.' And so that was that; I got my laugh, which, as I explained later to Sir Charles Cunningham, was all I had been after from the start.

Whatever Party may be in power, the machinery of government has to be kept turning over as smoothly and as efficiently as possible. In nearly thirty years of close connection with the organisation and management of a great political Party, I know that all Party leaders and their Chief Whips agree on this. I therefore came to Ministerial office with some knowledge of how best to relate my own work and responsibilities with those of the civil service. Top civil servants should not be unduly disturbed or nagged in their vitally important work which includes, *inter alia*, advice to their Ministers as to what is possible, what the alternatives are, and, where necessary, what is just not possible. If anybody wants to say here: 'But this is rule by the civil service', the answer is definitely 'No'—and I shall try to explain why.

The top civil servant furnishes his Minister with information as to the type of legislation that might be contemplated. The best example is probably the Finance Bill. A case can be submitted for an increase in Income Tax or in the Spirit and Tobacco Duties in order to produce the estimated rise in revenue required to meet expenditure, based on the Government's promises (partly vote-catching promises, maybe) to the electorate. The Minister—in this case the Chancellor of the Exchequer—has to choose the rope by which he prefers to take the risk of hanging himself, but it is the Treasury and the Inland Revenue who have worked out in advance which ropes are likely to be reliable, however unpopular, and which are worthless. (If the Minister fails in Parliament, not only he but his Government may hang.)

Political parties will, of course, disagree and fight about the size and brand of rope chosen by any Chancellor of the Exchequer. He has to convince himself that he is capable of forcing the probably unpalatable medicine down the throats of his own so-called supporters.

The civil servant has made no election pledges and therefore has none to implement, nor does he insist on 'selling' any particular line to a Minister. He will simply put before his Minister a series of alternatives. No Minister need be an expert within his particular department. But he must take the decisions. I was fortunate in my civil service advisers at the Scottish Office, headed throughout my period there by Sir David Milne as Permanent Under-Secretary of State.

It is an arduous job being Secretary for Scotland, involving constant travelling from and to London. Regularly my timetable involved leaving the Commons for King's Cross about midnight on Thursday, so as to be able to be at work in St Andrews House, Edinburgh, about 10 a.m. on Friday. I would often have to spend a night in Glasgow before returning to London on the overnight train on Sunday night. Even worse, the week-end could involve not only Thursday and Sunday nights in the train, but also one of the intervening nights in a cold, strange bed in Glasgow and the other in, say, Aberdeen.

I would not dream of claiming any spectacular achievements for Scotland, but looking back it pleases me to have done my best for the country for over five years and there are individual events which stand out in my memory. For example, it was something, I felt, to get Cabinet approval at last for the building of the Forth Road Bridge, which I announced personally in the House.

The Socialists, even when we were still in office, objected to my being invited to drive the first pile in the Firth of Forth at Port Edgar, South Queensferry, but what did such silly political nonsenses matter so long as one got the Bridge, which, incidentally, I was by no means certain of achieving. However, rather to my surprise, Lord Salisbury backed me up with energy and the Chancellor of the Exchequer expressed his approval—subject to a toll. Since the cost of crossing the Forth from North to South Queensferry by ferry with an ordinary car was 7s. 6d., not including passengers other than the driver, I was ready to agree to a toll of 5s. After some years of argument, this has been whittled down to 2s. 6d.—wrongly in my view. If one could save time—apart from the irritation and frustration that using the old ferry frequently caused—who, I argued, could object to paying 5s. for the use of a bridge on which fifty m.p.h. or more is normal?

I still believe I was right—and a 5s. toll would, obviously, pay off the cost of the undertaking in half the time; however . . .

During 1956, while I was at the Scottish Office, I had a curious and interesting experience. The Russian leaders Marshal Bulganin and Mr Khrushchev came to London on an official visit to see, in particular, the P.M. (Eden) and the Foreign Secretary. A lot of entertaining was laid on for them and while I don't know whether they enjoyed the visit or not they were certainly never allowed an idle moment.

They returned the hospitality showered on them by entertaining the entire Cabinet to lunch at the Russian Embassy, a vast Victorian mansion in Kensington Palace Gardens—or Millionaire's Row. I was present and had a lunch which should have satisfied any gourmand; unlimited caviare of more than one type and unlimited champagne, both pink and yellow.

After luncheon I was in a sitting-room with Anthony Eden and the Russians when it was agreed that they should pay a flying visit to Scotland and that I should escort them round Edinburgh and anywhere else which time would permit. Some Ministers had to leave to answer questions in the House and Eden asked me to stay on to keep him company, which I did. We were drinking some curious (Russian) brandy on a sofa when suddenly a flashlight went off and I realised we had been photographed. I said to Bulganin, through his interpreter, 'If a picture appears of me drinking brandy here at three o'clock in the afternoon, I shall lose my seat.' He sent for the photographer at once and some harsh words ensued—or so it sounded to my ears. I only hope that the poor photographer did not suffer too severely because, in fact, I was enjoying the brandy, doubtful though its bouquet was.

A few days later we flew from London to Edinburgh and never have I been driven so furiously through London. This was in order to keep up with our guests, who were led by about a couple of dozen police on fast motor bicycles. On the plane we had drinks and, I may add, the consumption of Scotch whisky went on throughout the day. I am sure that neither of our guests knew any English because their expressions never changed except when I uttered the one word 'whisky'; then they brightened up and smiled at once. They loved it, and certainly used it that day, and I had a case of it put on the return plane—at the taxpayers' expense—when they left Scotland.

They displayed great interest in all they saw of our Scottish capital and its surroundings but asked where all the heather was. I explained that there were masses of it further north and to the west, which they could have seen if we had had time to go on, but that the country around Edinburgh itself was agricultural—some of the best and richest in Britain.

I took them down to the Forth (railway) Bridge, where the Provost of South Queensferry greeted them and gave them two bottles of whisky, which produced more smiles. Khrushchev asked me why I had taken them to the Bridge; I told him because it was of no military importance and, anyhow, that the Germans had failed to hit it in two wars. If you fly over it, as I have done, you look down on a target resembling a razor's edge.

I had given no thought to the route we followed, except that it was the most convenient for our purpose, but the Russian leaders were impressed by the excellence of our roads and obviously thought that I had chosen only the best. I tried to convince them that this was not so and offered to direct the driver to take any secondary road or go wherever they wished.

They also commented on the service roads to the farms and I explained that, apart from the west coast, where one might have to resort to a boat, any farmer in the land could, to the best of my knowledge and belief, drive an ordinary motor-car right up to his own door. This too impressed them.

Coming back into Edinburgh they asked about housing, and here again they were apparently convinced that I had deliberately taken them via some of our best, if not most beautiful, developments. I explained that most of the better houses they saw had probably been built after the First World War, in the 1920s and 30s, but that others had been built since the end of the Second World War, in other words in the last ten years. I promised I was hiding nothing and that I would drive them down the Royal Mile, from Edinburgh Castle to Holyrood, and they could see some of our oldest houses, bordering the High Street and Canongate.

It began to rain a little and we had a slight skid. I told the interpreter, a young man from the Foreign Office, to assure them that my driver was good and reliable and that he had driven me safely for the past four years or so. Khrushchev replied, via the interpreter, that *he* had had the same driver for twenty-six years. I answered that it would be wise to make a change since his driver must by now know where too many of the bodies were buried. He laughed a lot and obviously didn't mind in the least.

I don't know whether it is a popular opinion nowadays but I believe this tough, undistinguished-looking man did as much as any man in his time to preserve the peace of the world and to calm international relations. Bulganin was the senior of the two but Khrushchev was the driving force. Bulganin was a superior, good-looking type, while Khrushchev was ungainly, ugly and untidy. I would have liked to give him a decent overcoat and a good pair of shoes.

It had already been a long day and it was not yet over, so I parted from them with relief at Holyrood Palace for a couple of hours' rest. The Lord Advocate (now a Judge, Lord Milligan) took over to give them tea while I retired to the New Club in Princes Street. I rejoined them to go to dinner at the Castle. After we had driven through three heavy iron gates I told

Khrushchev not to worry as we had no intention of locking them up. This little joke went down well too.

They enjoyed our smoked salmon (and more whisky) and Khrushchev asked me whether pollution of our salmon rivers worried me, because he was worried by it and its effect on the sturgeon and their precious roes, or caviare. I assured him that I was, and I implored him to safeguard his sturgeon most carefully against it.

At dinner, Bulganin asked me how long I suggested he should speak for, and I said for as long as he wished. He asked how long *I* would take, and I replied that my few words of introduction were cut and dried and should take the inside of two minutes. He smiled and asked me how it would be if he took a minute and a half. I said it wouldn't do at all because everyone present knew me and had no desire to hear me; they had all come to hear him. His speech lasted for some thirty-five minutes, which was about right since he had to speak one sentence at a time in Russian and then wait for the interpreter to repeat it in English.

After dinner we drove straight out to Turnhouse airfield and I saw them aboard their plane for London; it had been a tiring day, but interesting—and amusing.

When the time came for me to leave the Scottish Office I decided that, as a token of my gratitude and friendly feelings towards my colleagues—and, I would emphasise, not as a matter of routine *nor* at the taxpayers' expense!—I would give them a dinner party at the North British Hotel in Edinburgh, a place with fond memories for me dating back to my First World War days with the Royal Scots.

With the aid of my friend (and P.U.S.) Sir David Milne, a list of between thirty and forty guests was drawn up—heads of departments, under-secretaries, law officers, and personal private secretaries. There were a few speeches, including admirable ones by Sir David Milne and Sir Charles Cunningham (now Permanent Under-Secretary at the Home Office), the two men upon whom I had relied constantly for the best advice in the land. As our evening was drawing towards its (I hope) happy ending—I know I had been almost in tears a good deal of the time, if that denotes a happy end—Sir David leant towards me and said, 'I think we must give Rush his head.' I was rather against the idea of yet another speech but David assured me that he would 'not be long'.

Rush was my second private secretary and an admirable young man for whom I always had a high regard; he seemed to understand me—mysteriously—and was intelligent enough to avoid argument and to regard me as quite worthy of mirth when I lost my temper. I well remember, early in his days with me, saying to him at about 7 p.m. or so, 'Rush, if you bring in any more letters to sign I'll knock your —— head off.' This relieved me and seemed to entertain him, and on that basis we became friends.

To return to the dinner, Rush rose to his feet and spoke. After a minute and a half of this truly admirable speech, I whispered to David, 'He's been burning the midnight oil.' 'It's all right,' David replied. 'He won't be long now.' And, sure enough, Rush suddenly stopped, saying, 'Well, I'd better sit down now. If I don't my ex-boss will be saying "Now then, Rush, you push off"—as he used to say to me in the office, except that he didn't say "push".' Much applause, and the speech of the evening!

I must step a little out of time-sequence to include my last Scottish story. It happened soon after I resigned office but of course was still an M.P. and, what is more important in this context, a P.C.—or Privy Councillor.

I have only been shot twice in my life and both times as a civilian. The first time my father-in-law lodged a pellet in the back of my left hand, and it is still there. The second occasion had more interesting repercussions. I was shooting in my home county of Moray, beside Loch-in-dorb. I was in the bottom butt, nearest the loch, and there were quite a lot of grouse, but I scored one only because, as the second covey came near, the gun on my right decided to shoot between the flanker on my left and me. There was not enough room and I was waiting to shoot behind. I had my gun raised and ready, but the next thing I knew was a flash and the shot ripped into my face at about thirty-five yards range. I got about sixteen pellets in my face (luckily below my right eye, but in my cheek and lips) and also in both thumbs. Six still remain in my cheek and chin and three or four in my thumb and one hand.

A couple of days later I was telephoned by the Queen's secretary at Balmoral and asked if I could attend a Privy Council. He explained that I would make up the necessary quorum and that if I could not attend they would have to fly somebody up from London. My right cheek was covered with sticking plaster and I could not shave properly, but whether I was a pretty sight or not seemed a secondary consideration, so I agreed.

The secretary very considerately asked me if I was sure that they were not spoiling a day's shooting for me. I was able to reply. 'Don't worry at all about that, I've been shot already.' I explained what had happened and also that I feared I would not look very tidy.

I was invited to lunch so I drove the seventy miles over the hills from my home and arrived at Balmoral in good time because I wanted to have an opportunity of apologising to the Queen for my appearance. She could not have been more kind or sympathetic. She wanted to know·all about the incident and I explained briefly that as I was bleeding a lot, I had driven myself, followed by my sister Hermione Buller, who was with me in my butt at the time of the accident, to the hospital in Forres where a doctor extracted most of the shot and then gave me another kind of shot—of penicillin, which, I remarked, hurt about as much as the original.

The Queen then asked me what I did next and I told her the truth. I sent my sister home to Findhorn to explain things to my wife, including the fact that I might look a bit shop-soiled or odd when I arrived. Then I drove myself to the nearby Cluny Hill Hotel in Forres because, I explained, I felt in need of a 'small refreshment' or restorative. What, the Queen asked, did a 'small refreshment' mean? 'Ma'am,' I replied, 'in Scotland it means a double whisky.' Immediately she said, 'But do you think you should have had that after the penicillin?' My answer was straight off the cuff and uttered before I could stop it. I said, 'You know, Ma'am, that's exactly what the barmaid in Forres said.'

I would not be telling this story if I did not know that the

Queen herself told it to several people. When I next saw the then P.M. (Harold Macmillan) he knew all about it and asked me what I meant by comparing the Queen with my barmaid friend in Forres. I told him it was just something that had popped out of my mouth, but I added that when he next saw H.M., as he did practically every week, I would be obliged if he would tell her, with my compliments and humble respects, that the young lady behind the bar in Forres 'is a very nice girl too'.

Some time later there was a curious aftermath to my shooting accident. I had a bad cough and a doctor friend of mine at St George's Hospital, fearing that it might be cancer of the lung, arranged for me to have my chest X-rayed. I did this and my friend reported to me that I was in the clear, but he added, 'They are mystified by half a dozen or so black spots in your chin and neck.' Everybody was relieved when I was able to explain that the spots were, of course, the remaining No. 6 shot which had not been extracted a few years earlier because, as they were not bothering me, I decided to 'leave them be'; and there they remain.

XIX

It was during my time at the Scottish Office—in April 1955—
that Winston Churchill decided to resign the Premiership—
though not from Parliament—at the age of eighty. There was no
question as to who would succeed him. From the time he became
Prime Minister in 1940 he had regarded Anthony Eden as his heir.
Eden has said that the position of 'crown prince' was 'not necessarily enviable in politics' but he now came into his own at last.

He sought a dissolution almost at once and we went to the
country in May and obtained a majority of sixty, a sufficient
increase to enable him to carry on with reasonable security.

But such was not to be the case for long, and nothing could
have been more unexpected than the not-far-off 'coming events',
which failed even to cast their shadow before most people, including
myself.

Things appeared to be going well. Eden himself said of that
time: 'Employment was at a very high level, the balance of pay-
ments for once was giving no trouble and electorally the tide
appeared to be with us.' We had completed a million new houses
since 1951. Macmillan had now gone to the Treasury in place
of Butler, who became Lord Privy Seal in order to lead the House,
and Selwyn Lloyd had taken over the Foreign Office from Eden.

I have deliberately refrained from referring to the various
foreign problems which blew up with regrettable frequency and
in each of which there is material for a separate book. Berlin
and Western Germany remain with us; Cyprus cannot be said to be
settled. Kenya also was a cause for grave anxiety and absorbed
more of our scarce supply of troops, as does Aden today. But
what affected me personally as a member of the Eden Government
was the trouble over Egypt and the Canal.

Here the new Prime Minister became seriously involved in
the old Arab-versus-Jew troubles, which are apparently endless.

To recall the situation briefly, after the withdrawal of British troops from the Canal Zone there was no one left to keep order and nothing to stop hostile influences from filling the gap we had left behind us. The P.M. had naturally tried all sorts of negotiation and mediation when Nasser suddenly announced his decision to nationalise the Suez Canal and in so doing broke his agreements with us concerning, *inter alia*, the use of the Canal.

Then, only a matter of weeks later, Israeli forces moved into the Sinai peninsula. We, with the French, demanded at once that all troops must be withdrawn ten miles from the Canal, but Nasser rejected this. With the French, we launched an attack on 31 October 1956, capturing Port Said and moving along the Canal with the intention of separating the Jewish and Arab forces and safeguarding the Canal. The joint military operation was carried out most efficiently and with complete success, much credit being due to the effectiveness of the French paratroopers.

But the immediate effect of all this was an outcry of monumental proportions in many quarters of the globe, in addition to the Labour Party, led by Gaitskell, at home. Indeed few even in the Commonwealth stuck by us except Australia, and we were pilloried as aggressors. Our relations with America sank very low, while in the Commons there was a perpetual brawling and shouting match between the Labour Party and ourselves which was, to say the least of it, gravely worrying, and an exhausting strain on all.

The strain on the P.M., who was not at all well, was too great, but I have never witnessed a finer display of loyalty and enduring support than that which his new Foreign Secretary, Selwyn Lloyd, gave him. When the noise of the House allowed him to speak, he did so courageously and forcefully; and he had to repeat the effort constantly.

But in my own case the breaking point came when the P.M. announced suddenly that our forces, and the French, were to be withdrawn forthwith. We were only part of the way down the Canal and could have gone on to Suez without trouble.

I did not object to our going IN: what I did object to was our coming OUT.

I had to tell the P.M. of this privately and I did so in vigorous terms. His answer was that our objective had been achieved—namely the 'cease fire' between Arab and Jew—so that there was no excuse for going ahead. I explained that in my view it was right to go on because we had to make the 'cease fire' really effective, and if we and the French withdrew there could be no guarantee of its effectiveness.

I believe my argument to have been sound, but Eden had given his consent to withdrawal so there was no more to be done. It did, however, break my political heart and I was glad when it became possible for me to quit the Government in the following year. I had lost interest and was tired.

Certainly a military defeat had been inflicted on Nasser, and he deserved that for his breaches of faith, but because of our mishandling of the crisis he finished up stronger than he had been before; he is still the Head of his State and retains the Canal. I believe that the French also were upset and disgruntled—and I do not blame them.

Winston Churchill, after his retirement, never interfered with his successor and never expressed a view unless asked, but I know that he was gravely disturbed by the Suez venture. Someone must have told him of the strong views I held and which I had expressed both in writing and verbally to the P.M. A few days after it was all over Winston lumbered into my room in the Commons and slumped down into the only armchair, looking like a rather unhappy hippopotamus. He never mentioned a name, nor did he even refer specifically to Egypt or the Canal. All he said was, 'You were quite right.' I thanked him, saying that I hoped at the time that he might agree with my view. He sat thinking in silence for about a couple of minutes, then heaved himself up and stumped away again, without another word.

About two years later, when I was out of office, I found myself placed next to Mrs Eleanor Roosevelt at lunch. She was a lady of great force of character who did not hesitate to speak her mind. Straight away she said, 'You may be wondering what I think of you people over Suez. To clear the air I'll tell you. I was with you, and if my husband had been alive and your Winston Churchill had been in office, they would never have allowed that drift apart in our relations to happen.'

I am afraid that the whole venture was intended to be a one-man achievement by the great Foreign Secretary as a brilliant new Prime Minister, who would as a result be crowned with a wreath of laurel leaves and go down in history as a hero. Sad to say, thorns took the place of laurels.

Some years earlier, when we were in Opposition, Churchill suddenly asked me why I didn't like 'my Anthony'. The question no doubt arose from some criticism I had made, because at that time—as deputy Opposition leader—he was having to speak in debates on economics, housing, fuel, education and the rest. I answered Winston by explaining that while Eden might be first-class at the Foreign Office I feared that he lacked knowledge of other important matters such as I have mentioned. Churchill looked at me solemnly and merely said, 'Well, you'll have to have him.' I knew that his choice of his successor as P.M. had long been fixed on Eden, and have him we did, though, as it turned out, not for long. It must be said in fairness, however, that he did win a good General Election for us and bettered our very small 1951 majority under Winston.

My old regiment, the Royal Scots, was the last out of Suez and they did me the honour of inviting me to take the salute on their regimental day at Pinefield, Elgin, while I was still in office and they had only recently come home from Egypt. After the formal parade I was entertained in the Sergeants' Mess and then in the Officers' Mess for lunch where I had interesting talks with a number of serving soldiers who had been in Port Said. Naturally I led them on a bit and asked a few pertinent questions to which I received prompt and unequivocal answers. They were at a loss to understand why they had been ordered out of Port Said after going in so successfully and executing their orders with little trouble.

They told me that there was nothing to stop them going rapidly on to the end of the Canal and that there was no opposition worth bothering about—in fact none at all after they were clear of Alexandria and Port Said. One officer said that they could have done it blindfolded, to which another added 'and walking backwards'. They had two slight casualties from shell splinters and one senior company commander shot dead through the head by an unlucky shot from a sniper.

I asked if they regarded the whole expedition as a mistake and if they regretted it in any way. I was surprised by the answer, which was simply of the 'do or die' school. They never referred to the political side or to the rights or wrongs of it: the answer given by a senior officer was that they were glad to have carried out the operation because it showed the Reservists that they had some use for them, there being nothing more irritating for Reservists who had had to leave their civilian jobs than to be called up and then have nothing to do.

In January 1957, Anthony Eden's brief, inglorious Premiership came to an end; his health had broken down and he resigned. What part the Suez affair played in this we shall never know. Contrary to the usual practice, he left without tendering any advice to the Throne as to his successor. The obvious competitors were Harold Macmillan and R. A. Butler. After much anxious hurrying to and fro and conferring, with Lords Salisbury and Kilmuir busily counselling and counting heads, Harold Macmillan was sent for and undertook to form a new government.

It is always a help to an incoming Prime Minister to have a few vacant offices so that he can introduce new blood. Moreover, the new P.M., knowing me well, as he had for thirty years, was aware that after nearly six years at the Scottish Office I was looking for something less arduous, or preferably retirement. Certainly at sixty I was not 'new blood' and, worse still, Harold was my brother-in-law by marriage. I suggested to him that if charges of nepotism ever came up he could refute the Press by pointing out that at least he had sacked me!

I was only expressing the strong view I have always held (and often expressed to Winston Churchill): my maxim is 'the right man for the job and to hell with nepotism'. I told Harold Macmillan more than once that his son Maurice deserved office and should not be denied it because he was the Prime Minister's son.

But for myself, I had now had thirty-four years in Parliament, twenty-two of them as, successively, Scottish Whip, Chief Whip, and Secretary for Scotland. I was not sorry when my resignation was accepted; the P.M. might express his regrets but I had none.

I remained in the House for another two years, content to represent my constituents and taking some satisfaction from the fact that I completed nearly thirty-six unbroken years of service to them. But my active life in the wider arena of politics really ended in 1957, and Suez was its final chapter.

I have not dwelt much in these pages on major world affairs so perhaps I may indulge myself in a final thought on this crucial episode which historians—which I am not—believe will hold an important place in the history of British parliamentary government.

The issue as I see it was wider than Suez itself. We had supported the United States in Korea with troops as well as politically and I believe that President Truman was courageous and right. That struggle cost the life of my daughter's young husband, among the many other casualties, but such tragedies cannot be avoided in war. The object was to oppose the spread of Communism, just as it is the aim of the U.S.A. in the East today—an object in which they have in principle our support. But have they more right to be there than we had to be in Egypt in 1956?

We aimed at proving to Nasser—as with the Kaiser in 1914 and Hitler in 1939—that treaties and international agreements must not be treated as mere 'scraps of paper'. The rule of law was at stake. It is true that we failed, but had we gone on, as we could have, we would have had something to show for our effort; our position would have been stronger and we would have gained in prestige.

In logic, I cannot see why we were wrong in Egypt if the Americans are right now in the hard battle they are fighting in Vietnam. Perhaps a historian of the future will explain it all later, but it won't help me any. I shall be dead.

❧ XX ❧

I will not mind if I am credited with modesty for ending my story before the present decade began. But in truth the reason is that I am anxious to avoid the danger of anticlimax which follows retirement. However, as Winston Churchill was the greatest influence—and knowing him intimately the most memorable experience—in my life, I shall conclude with a last, brief note on him.

Although, as I said earlier, I did not know him until I was in my thirties, I knew *about* him and indeed I must have developed a particular interest in him quite early, because among the few newspaper cuttings I have preserved is a short leading article from the *Scotsman* at the time of his resignation as First Lord of the Admiralty in 1915. I was eighteen then, with no thought of politics, far less of ever working with Churchill, so he must have made a deep impression on me purely on the basis of what I had read or heard about him. If anybody should think, erroneously, from anything I have written, trying to be frank and fair, that I am a critic of Churchill, let them read this *Scotsman* leader of more than half a century ago and realise that the admiring boy who cut it out and kept it was, at the end, a devoted admirer of its subject:

'To his chequered political career it is needless to refer. Probably no man living has crowded more into forty-one years. He has seen service in five campaigns, he has written seven books, he has contested eight or ten strenuous elections, and he has occupied five different ministerial offices. The present episode cannot be regarded as more than a temporary interruption. With all his defects—and they are both many and obvious—he has brilliant qualities which need only a sounder judgment to make him a great political force. As a public speaker, given time for adequate preparation, he has few equals; and though as a Parliamentary debater he has hampered himself by trusting too largely on his notes, there have been occasions when he showed that that was a matter of habit rather than of necessity. His fellow-Radicals, while they have admired, have never trusted him wholly, for they suspected his fidelity to their principles. He has dealt too many harsh blows to have many friends among his political opponents. The minor acts, by which small men attract adherents, he has despised. None the less, he will have a good deal of sympathy in a resignation which involves him in no discredit, and constitutes no barrier to his future progress.'

Winston's birthday fell on St. Andrew's Day, 30 November, and a number of us Scots in London always dine together on that night. At these functions we sent him regularly for many years a message of greetings and good wishes, which I was always made to draft. I have beside me as I write an overnight telegram dated 2 December 1964, which reads: 'Thank you all so much, dear James.'

It was the last message I ever had from him, for he died within a few weeks.

When Evelyn Waugh died Christopher Sykes wrote: 'We never miss anyone so much as the friend who could make us laugh'; and he added that, for Waugh's friends, 'something precious, something quite irreplaceable, of warmth and colour has gone from our lives'. I made a note of this at the time, for I knew I could never express better my own feelings about Winston Churchill when he departed for ever from our lives.

INDEX

INDEX

Agar, Herbert and Barbie, 147
Aitken, Max, *see* Beaverbrook, Lord
Albert, King of Belgium, 28
Albert George, Prince (Duke of York, later George VI), 28, 42, 45, 48ff., 57
Ancaster, Earl of, 51
Andrews, Eamonn, 37
Asquith, Herbert (Earl of Oxford and Asquith), 70, 154
Astor, Nancy, Lady, 80–1
Atholl, Duchess of, 95
Attlee, Clement (Earl), 91–2, 118–119, 129, 136, 140, 142, 144, 145, 149, 150, 155, 156, 160, 164

Baldwin, Stanley (Earl Baldwin of Bewdley), xii, 2, 69ff., 74–82, 85, 95, 124, 132, 158
Baldwin, Mrs Stanley, 75
Balfour, A. J. (Earl of), 60, 71ff., 89
Bankhead, Tallulah, 59
Beaverbrook, Lord (Max Aitken), 89ff., 103, 119, 132ff., 136, 154, 157, 158
Beckett, Sir Rupert, 51
Berry, Commander, 21
Bevan, Aneurin, 143–4, 150, 160
Bevin, Ernest, 91, 100, 142, 155–7, 160
Blackburn, Lord, 40
Blair, Colonel P. J., 114
Bonham-Carter, Lady Violet, 154
Bowes-Lyon, Lady Elizabeth, 57, *see also* Elizabeth the Queen Mother, Queen
Bracken, Brendan, 89, 93, 100, 103, 106, 129
Brennan, Sergeant-Major, 21
Brett, Maurice, 36

Brett, Mrs Maurice, *see* Dare, Miss Zena
Briand, Aristide, 84, 85
Bridgeman, Willie, 158
Bridges, Sir Edward, 134
Brogden, Miss Gwendolyn, 35
Brook, Sir Norman, 134
Brooke, Sir Alan (Viscount Alan-brooke), 105, 129
Brown, John, 54
Buccleuch, Duke of, 124
Buchanan, George, 153, 154, 164
Buchan-Hepburn, Patrick (Lord Hailes), 102, 147
Buckmaster, Captain Herbert, 67
Bulganin, Marshal, 168, 170, 171
Buller, Hermione, 173
Butler, R. A., 139, 143, 175, 179
Byng, General, 24

Campbell-Bannerman, Sir Henry, 88, 109
Campion, Sir Gilbert, 152
Camrose, Viscount, 124
Canterbury, Archbishop of, 49
Carson, Sir Edward, 71, 73
Cavendish, Lady Dorothy, 47
Cavendish, Lady Moyra, 47
Cavendish, Lady Rachel, 47, 69
Cecil, Hugh, 145
Chamberlain, Sir Austen, 84, 85
Chamberlain, Joseph, 84
Chamberlain, Neville, xii, 2, 82–7, 96–8, 119
Chandos, Viscount, 100
Churchill, Winston S., xi, xii, xiv, 1, 2, 25, 28, 29, 34, 50, 71, 73, 77, 80, 82, 85, 87ff., 92–135, 136ff., 141, 144ff., 149ff., 155ff., 160ff. *passim*, 175, 177, 178, 181–2

Churchill, Mrs (Lady), 108
Churchill, Randolph, 101
Chute, Rev. J. C., 4
Cockburn, Lord, 41
Cooper, Gladys, 67, 68
Cooper, Lord, 165
Cork and Orrery, Earl of, 105
Cowdray, Viscount, 57
Crewe, Marquis of, 84
Cripps, Frederick, 91
Cripps, Sir Stafford, 91, 119-20, 142, 160
Cromwell, Oliver, 116, 136
Crookshank, Harry, 145, 161
Cumberland, Duke of, 55, 116
Cunningham, Sir Charles, 165, 166, 171

Dalton, Hugh, 155
Dare, Miss Zena, 36-7
Davidson, Sir John, 29ff.
Deverell, Major-General Cyril, 18, 20, 23
Dill, Sir John, 105
Disraeli, Benjamin, 82, 159
Dolly, Jenny and Rosie, 59, 67
Douglas-Home, Alec (Lord Dunglass, later Lord Home), 83, 98, 158, 162
Dugdale, Tommy (Lord Crathorne), 89, 92, 93, 163
Dyson, Colonel, 11, 13, 17

Eden, Sir Anthony (Lord Avon), xii, 2, 84, 89, 91, 99, 115, 129, 139, 146, 147, 156, 157, 168, 175ff.
Edward VII, King, 44
Edward, Prince of Wales (King Edward VIII, later Duke of Windsor), xii, 28, 44, 46, 49, 74, 75, 81, 82, 132
Eisenhower, Dwight D., 25
Elizabeth II, Queen, 164, 173, 174
Elizabeth the Queen Mother, Queen, 40, see also Bowes-Lyon, Lady Elizabeth

Elliott, Walter, 143, 164
Esher, Viscount, 36

Fisher, Baron, 88
FitzRoy, Mr Speaker (later Lord Daventry), 151
Foch, Marshal Ferdinand, 25, 26

Gaitskell, Hugh, 144, 160, 176
Galbraith, Tom (Lord Strathclyde), 163
Gaulle, General Charles de, 25, 90
George V, King, xii, 43, 44ff., 53, 56
George VI, King, 82, 164, see also Albert George, Prince
George, Prince (later King George IV), 55
George, Prince (Duke of Kent), 45
Gerrard, Teddy, 59
Gilmour, Sir John, 78
Gladstone, W. E., 137, 155, 159
Gloucester, Duke of, see Henry, Prince
Gough, General, 22, 24
Grant, Sir Ludovic, 39
Greenwood, Arthur, 91
Greig, Louis, 28, 42, 45, 46, 48
Greville, Mrs Ronald, 71, 72
Greville, Sir Sidney, 50, 57
Grey, Sir Edward, 5
Grigg, P. J. (Sir James), 102
Guise, Duc de, 2
Guise, Marie de, 2

Haig, Sir Douglas, xii, 10, 22, 24ff., 29ff.
Halifax, Earl of, see Wood, Edward
Hallam, Basil, 35
Hamilton, Claud, 44
Harris, Sir Charles, 89, 91, 152
Harrison, Rex, 35
Harvie-Watt, George, 104
Heath, Edward, 117
Henry VIII, King, 2
Henry, Prince (Duke of Gloucester), 45

Herbert, A. P., xii, 117–18
Himmler, Heinrich, 128
Hitler, Adolf, 34, 76, 83, 85, 95, 180
Hogg, Quintin, 98
Holloway, Stanley, 35
Home, Earl of, 162, see also Douglas-Home, Sir Alec
Hoover, President H. C., 58
Horne, Lord (Sir Robert), 40, 78

Ismay, General Lord, 100, 131

James V, King of Scotland, 2
Jeffreys, Colonel (General Lord Jeffreys), 108
Joe, oil driller, 63ff.
Joffre, Marshal Joseph, 31
John, Augustus, 92
Julius Caesar, 86

Kaiser, the, see Wilhelm II of Germany
Kent, Duke of, see George, Prince
Keyes, Nelson, 35
Kilmuir, Earl of, 179, see also Maxwell Fyfe, David
Kirkwood, David, 153
Kitchener, Earl, 6, 30
Khrushchev, Nikita, 168ff.

Lancaster, Osbert, 144
Lauder, Harry, 35
Law, Andrew Bonar, 69, 73, 154
Lawrence, Sir Herbert, 29
Leathers, Fred (Viscount Leathers), 111
Leicester, Lady, 48
Linklater, Eric, 34
Lloyd, Selwyn, 175, 176
Lloyd George, David, 25, 32, 70, 73, 124, 154
Locker-Lampson, Commander, 128
Ludendorff, Erich von, xii, 29
Lumsden, Major A. F., 17ff., 22, 26
Lyttelton, George, 3

Lyttelton, Oliver (Lord Chandos), 105

MacDonald, Ramsay, 70, 142, 153
McKenna, Reginald, 73
Macleod, Iain, 143
Macmillan, Harold, 47, 91, 105, 163, 164, 174, 175, 179
Macmillan, Maurice, 179
Margesson, David, 75, 77, 78, 80, 82, 88, 89, 92, 148, 150
Marples, Ernest, 163
Mary, Princess (later Queen Mary I of England), 2
Mary, Princess Royal, 45, 46, 52
Mary, Queen, 47, 54
Mary Queen of Scots, 2
Maudling, Reginald, 143
Maxton, James, xii, 83, 86, 141, 151ff.
Maxwell Fyfe, David (Lord Kilmuir), 105, 115, 179
Melbourne, Lord, 162
Milligan, Lord, 170
Mills, Viscount, 163
Milne, Sir David, 166, 171, 172
Molotov, V. S., 130
Molyneux, Sir Richard, xii, 50–3
Montgomery, Viscount, 51
Moran, Lord, 100, 101, 145
Moray, 1st Earl of, 2
Moray, 12th Earl of, 55
Moray, 17th Earl of, 3
Moray, Randolph, Earl of, 41
Morrison, Herbert, 104, 142, 144, 149, 150
Mumford, Mr, 118
Murray, Barbara, 58
Mussolini, Benito, 34

Nabarro, Gerald, 65
Napoleon, 4, 97
Nasser, Colonel, 176, 180
Nivelle, General, 20, 31
Nugent, Tim (Lord Nugent), 5

Ogilvy, Bruce, 44

Palmer, subaltern, 21
Pétain, Marshal Philippe, 20, 25, 32
Pickthorn, Sir Kenneth, 80
Pitman family, 40
Plastiras, General, 103
Plumer, General, 32
Ponsonby, General John, 26
Pope Pius XII, 129
Profumo, John, 33

Raeburn, Sir Henry, 41
Redmayne, Martin, 80
Richardson, H. E., 39
Roosevelt, Mrs Eleanor, 177
Rosebery, Earl of, 137
Rosebery, Eva, 121
Rowan, Leslie, 100, 121
Rush, private secretary, 172

Salisbury, 3rd Marquis of, 159
Salisbury, 5th Marquis of, 91, 162,
    168, 179
Sefton, Earl of, 50, 52
Seymour, Sir Reginald, 50
Shawcross, Sir Hartley, 140
Sitwell, Dame Edith, 2
Slessor, Sir John, 143
Snadden, William McNair, 95
Stalin, Joseph, 119, 129, 130
Stanley, Oliver, 115, 139
Stephen, Rev. Campbell, 151, 154
Stevenson, Robert Louis, 27, 40
Stonor, Sir Harry, 50, 53, 54
Strathmore, Earl of, 40
Stresemann, Gustav, 85
Stuart, Prince Charles Edward, 55,
    116

Stuart, Francis, 3, 58, 161
Stuart, John, 28
Sturt, Napier (Lord Alington), 59
Sykes, Christopher, 182

Taylor, H. B. (Labour Whip, 1945),
    141
Thomas, Godfrey, 44
Thomson, Sir Frederick, 78
Tree, Ronald, 106
Truman, President Harry S., 180
Tuck, Alec, 58ff.
Tuck, Hallam, 58

Vanderbilt, Mrs Cornelius, 59ff.
Vaughan, H. M., 2
Vesey, Colonel Thomas, 51
Victoria, Queen, 54, 55, 153, 162

Wakefield, Sir Wavell, 80
Walker, Sir Alexander, 113
Waugh, Evelyn, 182
Wavell, Earl, 51
Westminster, Duke of, 98
Wheatley, John, 153, 154
Whiteley, Will, 91, 139, 141, 142
Wigram, Sir Clive, 56
Wilhelm II of Germany (Kaiser),
    34, 86, 180
Wilson, Harold, 85, 160
Windsor, Duke of, see Edward,
    Prince of Wales
Winterton, Earl, 104
Wood, chauffeur, 49, 50
Wood, Edward (Earl of Halifax),
    74, 87, 97
Woolton, Earl of, 163

York, Duke of, see Albert George,
    Prince